Extraordinary Moments in an Ordinary Life

For Lux + Nye,
Love Janet

Janet Heartson

Extraordinary Moments in an Ordinary Life

Janet Heartson

Railroad Street Press
St. Johnsbury, Vermont

Copyright © 2011 Janet Heartson

Cover: *The Maiden* © 2011 Ed Hall

ISBN 9781936711192

Credentials

MA Psychology & Spirituality

Certified Kinesiologist

Certified Practioner of NLP

Certified Reiki Master

Verified Shaman

All rights reserved. No part of this book may be reproduced, stored in a retrieval system, or transmitted in any form or by any means, without the prior written permission of the publisher, except in the case of brief quotations embedded in critical articles or reviews.

For additional copies of this book please visit www.heartsons.com

Railroad Street Press
394 Railroad Street, Suite 2
St. Johnsbury, Vermont
(802) 748-3551

Acknowledgements

I want to thank the Universal Life Force for providing this life of miracles. Thanks also to Barbara Williams for her coaching and editing and formatting without her I would have procrastinated myself right out of printing this. Marcie Pleasants was the first to edit this and laugh and cry along with me and my stories. Jen Smith edited it again later on when I had added more. I have had a lot of help with this book. Thanks to Ed Hall, photographer extraordinaire, for his beautiful photograph. His photo is on my cover. Ed's website is www.hallcroftphoto.com. Many thanks to all those who contributed to the synchronicities by showing up and being themselves.

Table of Contents

Navigating Your Own Extraordinary Moments

Introduction

"...The transcendental experience is more real than the world of the senses." Deepak Chopra

It is becoming more common to hear about healing, raising ones vibrations and intuitive guidance. Many of us cultivate these experiences and attributes and some of us were born with them. I am of the latter group.

My inner landscape includes non-ordinary realities that are common with shamans and mediums. This book describes some of the peak moments in my life, the miracles that have come my way by the grace of the divine. These experiences punctuate my journey of self-discovery. Please join me while I recount some of my unusual travels. My hope is that in sharing these extraordinary moments, the reader may become more open to their own. Perhaps these stories will open some doors that have been waiting for you to walk through. I hope that my openness will inspire more fulfillment and healing.

It seems inevitable that I would become a writer because I love to read. I enter into a new reality and try it on like an outfit in a store. I walk around and look at it from all angles in the mirror and decide if it makes sense for me. At other times, reading is like dipping my toes into a lake and getting a sense of whether or not I want to swim there. Or sometimes I dive right in, knowing that whatever I experience will make me feel more alive.

No matter how you approach this book, I think it will stir you. It may make you ponder reality. I guess my life has been a bit like a winding road, with unexpected twists and turns that lead to some extraordinary views.

This book comes with a blessing. May you experience your higher self through which many soul adventures come.

I also welcome the opportunity to assist you in your journey of self-discovery. I am a Life Coach and a Healer. I have developed a loving and effective healing process which uses a mix of Kinesiology, Neuro-Linguistic Programming, Psychology, Reiki, Shamanism and my intuitive abilities as the client needs them. I work in person or over the phone.

One of the reasons I have written this book is so people can get to know me a little and get an idea of what to expect when working with me. My biography (below) and my web site www.heartsons.com have more information about my healing practice.

Bio

My credentials are eclectic like my tastes. I have a certification in Neuro-Linguistic Programming (NLP). NLP techniques empower people to let go of limiting patterns and step into their greater potentials.

I have a Master's Degree in Spirituality and Psychology from Holy Names College in Oakland, California. These studies supported my belief that I couldn't help my clients get well without helping their Spirits as well as their minds and bodies. We were souls long before we entered these bodies in this lifetime. Healing happens most thoroughly when we acknowledge this.

I am a certified Kinesiologist. Kinesiology uses muscle testing to access issues that live in the body as unconscious or subconscious processes. We have repetitive behaviors that don't work for us and we can't understand why. I find the source of the issue through the use of kinesiology. I am able to be a compassionate detective, and take you to the time of the trauma that caused a short circuit in your system. The belief you developed based on the trauma can prevent you from acting in a positive way. Once it becomes conscious, we can heal it.

I am a Reiki Master. When I use Reiki with clients and loved ones, they begin to realign their own energies to facilitate healing. Reiki energy reinstates the flow through the meridians so the body can repair itself.

I make flower and gem essences. They have energetic blueprints that help our systems function more effectively. They are useful tools to correct subtle imbalances, much like homeopathic remedies. You can buy Bach Flower Remedies at your local health food store. I recommend always having Rescue Remedy on hand for those times when you need to realign your energy after an accident or frightening event. You can put a few drops in your dog or cat's water too if they have had a trauma.

I am a shaman. This means I can travel in non-ordinary reality and help you retrieve parts of you that you left behind due to trauma or extreme confusion. You'd be surprised how many people need support in this way.

I am also a Shape Shifter. I can enter the consciousness of an animal, insect, gem or flower to discover its energetic blueprint or essence. This is perhaps my most enjoyable skill. I have soared with eagles, run with deer, flitted with hummingbirds and communed with wolves. To experience another being, even for a moment, brings a bliss beyond words.

One thing I was delighted to discover was that, of all the creatures I've experienced, humans are the only ones that worry. How nice to know that other creatures are not burdened in that way! They have a purity of experience that is delightful to feel. Unless the animal has been domesticated and poorly treated, there are no issues of low self-esteem, judgment or despair. These are purely human traits, and I suspect if we got in touch with our own instincts we would leave some of these self-limiting issues behind.

I am also an Earth Steward. I feel Mother Earth's energies and I know my relationship with her is reciprocal. I owe her my loyalty, love and devotion. I would not exist without her generosity, and she flourishes with my care. If shape shifting is my most joyous experience, my saddest is when I feel the abuse that we humans perpetrate on Mother Earth. I can get caught up in that and feel great despair and shame for being part of a group that hurts her. But I remind myself that I make choices that nurture and that I must focus my energies on loving her.

Miracles are with us every day. We can experience them more readily if we keep an eye out for them, have an attitude of surrender, and if we acknowledge and respond appropriately to our emotions. There is a rhythm to miracles, a cyclic process that can get clogged when someone is afraid to fully express or experience emotions.

I am a clairsentient person. That means that I experience a sense of knowing that is beyond the five senses. This requires me to trust my Self-awareness rather than rely only on what I see or hear.

I consider telepathy the original language between mother and child in the womb and before words. Often, when we are required to communicate with words our telepathic connection unconsciously shuts down between parents and child, our telepathy gets put aside and can atrophy. It happens so innocently: a baby sends the telepathic message, "I'm awake, come get me." Then the mother thinks, "I should check on the baby," and then the phone rings, or dishes are almost done or she needs to finish a conversation so she waits before responding. Then the baby sends a stronger telepathic message, "Hey, come get me, I'm wet and feeling cranky and I want to be comforted." Mom feels the tug intuitively, but what is on the stove might burn if she doesn't get to it right away. The baby then cries and she comes running. The message the baby gets is, "My telepathy doesn't work and I get what I need if I cry," which later translates into, "I get what I want if I use words."

One of my greatest joys is reuniting individuals with their own telepathic abilities and teaching them how to use it. It is especially fulfilling when I have the opportunity to train parents to maintain this connection with their children. People often release a great deal of grief when they regain their telepathy. It is such a sweet communion, and the loss of it has been unconsciously eroding our happiness over a lifetime.

The disconnection with our telepathic abilities shows up with people's insecurity with words. Learning disabilities can be helped when people reclaim their telepathy. Words can be the object of our anger if we are mourning our ability to connect telepathically. This telepathic connection is a deep form of loving and our self esteem can be lowered when we lose it.

In maintaining telepathic communication with our children, we never lose the skill that will save our planet. If we feel oneness with all things, we make decisions based on connection, not separation. We evolve to a higher consciousness that knows we are all in this together and what we do to someone else reverberates back to ourselves. We become less oriented toward war and more focused on cooperation and love.

In her book, The Bond Lynne McTaggart researches our essential nature which is to bond and cooperate. I always love reading books that express what I deeply feel to be true. Bruce Lipton takes this tale to the cellular level with his book The Biology of Belief. I highly recommend their books.

I hope that you enjoy my book and the demonstrations of connectedness, biology and bonding.

Astral Projection into the Fly

"The universe is immense and gorgeous and magnificent. I salute it. Every speck, every fly on the window salutes the Universe. Every leaf has meaning. I think the Universe is expanding-it is experiencing and accomplishing. And we have the opportunity to add to its glow. Everybody can love, in the place where they are. In the physical body in which we are. In the life in which we are involved. We can all add our share of love without leaving the room." - Helen Nearing

I share my stories in the hope that they will teach you to accept miracles in your life. I write to express my love in a world that can be difficult and stressful to navigate. The following is a powerful memory from age five that will give you a sample of the wild journey of my life.

I didn't want to take a nap. I was fine without it and I sensed that Mom just wanted me out of her hair. I lay there staring at the ceiling and listening to a fly buzzing on the window screen. It was hot and I could feel beads of sweat on my forehead. Outside I heard birds and the steady drone of a table saw somewhere in the distance. The sound began to permeate my mind and I began to relax as I felt the vibrations move through me. My irritation turned into a peaceful surfing of sound.

Suddenly my body was filled with an electric joy that jolted me out of my dazed mood. I felt alive with energy and happiness in every cell. Something strange was happening. A giant square pattern appeared before me. As I puzzled over this, I realized I was looking at the window screen from close up. I had become the fly.

As soon as I had this thought, fear set in. Adrenalin raced through my body, wiping away the joyous feelings. I slammed into the bed as my awareness returned to my five-year-old body. I lay there stunned for quite a while as my mind and body processed the fear from the adrenalin and the shock of the experience.

Eventually, fear gave way to curiosity and excitement. I went over to the screen and watched the fly, realizing he and I had been one for a moment. I put my finger out and he walked onto my finger and we sat there together as friends. I wondered if he had experienced me for a while too. I wondered how that all had happened and if I could do it again.

I tried to relax and stared at the fly for a long while, trying to *will* the exchange to happen again, but it didn't. I was just me and I was very confused.

I never talked about this to my mother or anyone. Somehow I knew that the experience was a symptom of something that made me different and therefore unacceptable. I can't recall how my family had taught me not to share these things, but it was clear that I could not. From that day on, I felt alone in my experience and longed to connect with someone who understood me.

Soap Stone Memories

Perhaps as I think back before this, I may know what caused me to feel it was unsafe to share my "secrets". When my family watched the evening television like Jackie Gleason or the Ed Sullivan Show, I had a job I did. I had a special book, a heavy-duty file, a pile of special stones and a box. I would file down what I later discovered was soapstone, into a fine powder that I collected in the box.

Every evening I labored on this. No one knew why I did it and I got a fair amount of teasing about it from my older sisters. My parents would ask me questions about it and no answer I gave them made their concern go away. Not wanting to be the subject of their concern, I began to do things in private. It is painful to know that the people who love and protect you don't understand you. It is also painful to know that being yourself frightens them.

Years later when I visited the Miwok Indian Museum in Carmel, California, I discovered the source of my ritual. The natives used to make soap out of the stone and I believe I was having a past life memory. During that same trip, I recall looking at a painting of an old monastery and weeping. It depicted a time when Christian Missionaries tried to "rehabilitate" Native Americans using some barbaric techniques. They separated children from their families. They forced them to speak English instead of their native tongue. They made them wear shoes, which were uncomfortable compared to moccasins. And perhaps most intrusive was the forced separation from the land, its rhythms and wild beauty.

I certainly cannot prove that I lived a life amongst the Miwok Tribe, but my heart knows this truth that I discovered fifteen years after I stopped filing soapstone into powder.

"Grandfather,
Look at our brokenness.
We know that in all creation,
Only the human family
Has strayed from the Sacred Way.
We know that we are the ones
Who are divided,
And we are the ones
Who must come back together
To walk in the Sacred Way.
Grandfather,
Sacred One,
Teach us love, compassion and honor
That we may heal the earth
And heal each other." — *Ojibway people of Canada*

Dog and Dolphin

Family photo albums are filled with pictures of holidays, graduations and vacations. Most of my memories do not reflect my wearing of Easter bonnets or posing with relatives. The most memorable events in life often occur at times that no one would ever think to photograph.

I remember sitting on my father's lap while he cried about the men he killed in the war. This was WWII. I knew he had been drinking by the slur in his speech and the intensity of his agony. He'd say over and over again, "They were just boys like me. They were just boys like me! I had to kill them. The Nazis had to be stopped. They were just boys like me." When he was done repeating these phrases, they would echo in my six-year-old brain like the nagging sound of a mosquito in your ear at night. I became determined to help people whose pain repeated inside their souls to be able to feel compassion for themselves and find a way to heal. Of course that was also my own healing journey.

There are two miracle stories about animals and their gifts to humans from my Dad that I tell often. They are also in sharp contrast to the war and the pain my father suffered both physically and emotionally.

The young German Sheppard came to my father while he was in the first infantry division during WWII. He followed Dad and seemed determined to go wherever he went. Dad developed affection for the dog, but received protests from his fellow soldiers about it. There were arguments about not wanting to share rations with a dog, or that he might distract them, and that he was too much responsibility in the midst of war. Dad would try to drive the dog away, but the dog always came back. He finally convinced his regiment to keep the dog on a trial basis.

The dog won everyone's acceptance when he alerted them to Germans coming with his exceptional hearing. This happened several times, and so the dog was allowed to stay with my father.

One day they were in the trenches and things were looking bad. Dad was really scared as shots fell all around him. It was raining, and the trenches were muddy and cold. The Germans were getting closer and the ditches barely offered enough cover. A few of the men around him had been shot and the future was looking grim.

The dog was beside my father, quiet and alert. All of a sudden, his dog leapt up and took the bullet that was headed for Dad. He quietly died. Dad survived this battle and when he had a moment to reflect on his experience he became convinced that the dog had deliberately forfeited his life to save him.

I think this next WWII story entered my psyche and gave me an understanding of what it means to be connected to nature and how important it is to our survival.

My father was on ship in foreign waters on his way to another exhausting invasion. Being in the first infantry division, he was not fond of ships and had a tendency toward seasickness. He had already experienced the horror of diving into a school of jellyfish and barely living to tell the tale of a thousand stings. He was out of his element. He knew how to fix engines and traverse the land, but traveling by sea was not comfortable.

His ship was attacked from the air by German planes. The bombs spread fear and fire and death all around him. He was blown from the ship, which was left in pieces in a rocky sea. He saw no one left alive and began to swim blindly in the direction of a hoped-for shore. He swam for hours. Day became night and night returned to day and still he saw no land. His limbs were too tired to swim and hypothermia was taking over. He realized that he may as well surrender to the hopelessness of the situation as there was no adrenaline left to force his body to continue his search for safety.

He let go of the struggle and began to sink. Just before he lost consciousness he saw the eye of a dolphin. Miraculously he later woke up and found himself on shore. He dragged himself up the sand and away from the licks of the tide and began to collect himself. Slowly awareness returned of the ship and his solitary voyage to find safety. And then his last conscious memory came back, the beautiful eye of the dolphin as he sank into the sea. And he knew in his deepest soul that he owed his life to that dolphin.

Is it any wonder I have such a precious relationship with dolphins?

Dad's Motorcycle Accident

"The problem is how to be open enough and safe enough at the same time." — W. A. Mathieu, *The Listening Book*

By age eight I had learned not to ignore my "visions." One summer day, I suddenly knew that my Dad was in trouble, bleeding and unconscious in the field. I ran around telling adults to go find Dad because he was hurt and bleeding. I had seen that his nose was torn off. People thought it was absurd. But my neighbor, Michael, was a doctor and he had loaned his motorcycle to my Father. He no longer heard the sound of the motor in the field and realized that something could be wrong. Michael found him unconscious and bleeding from his nose, which was nearly shorn off.

My father had forgotten about the new fence along the interstate and he had run right into it. Michael ran back to the house and called the ambulance to bring him to the hospital. Dad was revived and his nose was sown back on.

No one said a word to me, not right after and not anytime later. Nothing! I got the message loud and clear by their silence that they could not handle my ability to know things even though it saved our Dad's life. How traumatic that was for me. I look back at that time as a time when I felt disoriented. I couldn't find my place or even my people.

My parents were very smart, and if they didn't understand, who would? It wasn't until I read a book by Carlos Castaneda that I began to know I wasn't alone. By age 11, I had begun to read anything I could get my hands on about Shamanism and Spirituality. I read Herman Hesse, Kahlil Gibran, The Seth books, Rudolph Steiner, Star Hawk, and the Bible. I began to realize everyone had experiences that they had difficulty understanding. Some were Shamanic like my own, some were emotional, some were archetypal, but they all caused us to question and explore what it meant to be here.

"I wanted only to live in accord with the promptings which came from my true self. Why was that so very difficult?" Hermann Hess, *Demian*. This phrase became a kind of mantra to me: his angst was my angst and we were in it together.

I am a life coach and Kinesiologist now. I use NLP, Reiki and my Shamanic abilities to facilitate healing with clients. I am grateful for the gifts that come through me and I know that my clients are to. One of the reasons for writing this book is to alert people to the ways they can support their children in understanding and maintaining their gifts. It is common for a client to come to me because these skills were stifled in their families and through the school systems.

We need these gifts in the world. We need to make heartfelt decisions that are in harmony with Mother Earth. We need to stand up for our rights against war and government controls that are out of control. I want to be free and I don't want to die because we have soiled our home too much to salvage it. That is why I share with you the *Extraordinary Moments in an Ordinary Life*. Blessings on your journey to your "True Self."

Akashic Records

I was a bright student with a high IQ and I loved to learn. I did, however, hate school. I felt constrained and bored and sometimes insulted by the curriculum and the attitude of some of the teachers. I know I must have been a handful because I loved to debate and wasn't a bit shy. I especially struggled with my history teacher. I questioned why we were expected to memorize the dates and facts around the wars, but weren't delving into the meaning or, more important, the prevention of them. I had some real fears about our society and wanted to keep brainstorming with others about what we could do to improve humanity. He was infuriated by my "poor attitude" and seemed relieved when I skipped class.

One day I was feeling especially hurt by our conflicted relationship and my general disappointment in school. I went into the field behind my house and lay in the grass sobbing. I cried until all my tears were spent. I felt exhausted and empty. I fell into a light sleep\meditation. A voice inside me said, "Let go, let go, let go." Those words were repeated over and over again like a mantra.

My awareness left my body and drifted up into the sky and beyond. Then I was in a great room filled with all the knowledge that existed and was able to absorb it all by simply thinking about it. I had the thought, "I wonder about..." and before I finished the thought, all the information about that subject would be instantly within me. It was not in my head, but permeated my whole cellular structure.

Then I became aware that I was experiencing something "weird" and zoomed out of the great room and back into the field. Later I read that others had experienced similar things and there was something called the Akashic Records. I was glad to know that I was not alone in this knowledge.

This experience taught me that all knowledge was within me and that books were a circuitous route at best. This experience gave me confidence in my thinking process and comfort in my quest for truth. The thought that truth existed within me was enormously healing for me. It quieted my spirit and gave me some trust in life.

Cosmic Joy

I was more aware of death than the average child. I drew empty swings and wrote poems about death and war and losses. I began to worry about my cat Cinders dying. I listened to a record of Romeo and Juliet every night before I went to sleep. There was tragedy brewing and I could feel it coming.

There is an ongoing disagreement in my family about when my mother's terminal diagnosis was made. I think it happened when I was ten, but everyone says it was five years later. I think the confusion comes from my own precognition. We are all correct. I knew when I was ten, and they officially found out five years later.

I would have been diagnosed as clinically depressed at that time if someone had noticed my chronic unhappiness. I would go off to brood in the woods or by my favorite brook, so no one noticed. One day I was so depressed I could do nothing but collapse into the field and cry. I cried for quite a long time and told "God" how disappointed I was in the world and how alone I felt. My heart ached so much I felt it could burst. Crying hard, I emptied myself. I didn't know what else to do.

Later, as I lay there exhausted and spent, the sound of the crickets began to penetrate my awareness. Then the smells of the earth beneath me wafted into my senses. A bird flew overhead and I felt the grace with which it moved. In the next instant, a palpable joy permeated my being. Every cell began to sing and a lightness entered me. I have never forgotten that celestial gift. Had I not received that moment of reprieve from pain, I don't know what would have become of me. It was a moment that changed my life forever.

Experiencing that moment of unlimited joy gave me the

awareness of the law of complementary energies. This is the natural law that states that for every yin there is a yang. Balance is natural, so when we feel overwhelmed by a thought or feeling, we can trust that the opposite feeling is also available to us. It's a dance of polarities and when we accept this dance we also transcend it. We can know that we are more than the simple reaction from one dynamic to another; we are greater than the polarized way of being. The qualities that enable us to transcend are faith and wisdom. Now when I am in deep despair, I need only remember how close joy is on the wheel of life.

Joan's Distress Call

At age 13, I regularly babysat for a family that I dearly loved. They took me with them on vacation in Florida to watch the children. One Saturday night I woke up at midnight having dreamed that my sister Joan had died. I had seen her scream and fly off from the family. The dream left me shaken and deeply disturbed. It had a potency that was unlike most dreams. I tried to let it go and forget it, but its presence in my psyche was unrelenting. Finally, I called my mother to ask about Joan. Joan lived with her husband and children about an hour away from my mother, but my mother reassured me that everything was fine. I tried to accept that and went about my work but the feeling persisted.

Finally when I returned home and could make the call, I asked Joan how she was and told her about my dream. She gasped and said that at midnight that Saturday she had been entertaining guests. She had little pizzas in her gas oven and when she had gone to remove them it had blown up in her face. At that moment she had thought she was dead. It turned out that all that had happened was that her eyebrows and lashes had burned, but Joan remembered thinking that she was dying in that split second of the explosion.

Somehow that thought of dying had traveled over two thousand miles to enter my awareness. I was able to let go of my worry for her then, but a new worry began: what was this phenomenon that I experienced and why had I experienced it? And what was I supposed to do if it happened again? Once again, my parents' dismissal of my experience taught me that they would not be useful resources. Some Christians judge psychic phenomena as if they are from negative forces. So I knew I could not go to my mothers' church community to find support. So I tried to forget it.

Looking back now, I wonder how my life would have been different if I'd had a mentor to guide me in this mysterious realm of consciousness.

I feel that these kinds of experiences are from a thread of love connecting us to our family and friends. How can that be considered evil? I do realize that we fear what we don't understand. Isn't it time to learn about these experiences of connection and allow them to take their rightful places in our lives?

Butterflies and Sunbursts

Mom used butterflies as a metaphor for life's transformations. These transformations are almost always painful in that we must dissolve away what we were in order to become the next beautiful thing that we are meant to be. It doesn't feel beautiful in the process though. We get attached to being the caterpillar or the cocoon and we have no foresight about what we are becoming. So we must let go and trust that the unknown is good. This takes faith.

During Mom's funeral a few things happened that made us feel as though she were conducting her own funeral in the same way she had conducted the church choir while she was living. It was September. She was to be buried in Williamstown, Vermont, where her relatives were buried. It was a gloomy day, which was fitting as it matched our hearts. We had a procession from White River to Williamstown. The exit off the highway took us from the top of a hill into the town in a valley. At the top of the hill, as we slowly made our way off the highway a large cloud opened and a shaft of light streamed down. The rays seemed to reach down and fill the cemetery with their light.

Mom used to say that when rays came down from clouds that it was a ladder letting someone into heaven. My sisters and I looked at each other and said simultaneously, "There goes Mom!" With our hearts a little lighter, we stood at the gravesite feeling curious about what next surprise she might have in store for us.

During the ceremony a butterfly landed on my arm and fluttered about my face. I was trying to concentrate and hold myself together and this butterfly was distracting me. Suddenly a sob caught in my throat and I realized that Mom was sending this butterfly to make sure I knew that this pain would pass. All of her children would have similar experiences with the butterfly. It wasn't until later when we talked about our graveside experiences that we realized she had done her magic for us all.

On her gravestone is a butterfly designed by my brother. How lucky we are to have memories of an insightful mother who makes the sun break through clouds and butterflies dance around her children. And she was wise enough to teach us to see the extraordinary in our ordinary lives.

Many years later I had another great butterfly experience. It was my third year on Maui. I was pining for my family and friends. I missed the longtime friends who had grown with me and accepted me in all my shortcomings and gifts. New friends can be good, but they don't know your history and they don't know how hard you've worked to get where you are now.

Nature is a good counselor for me, so I went for a walk on Thompson Road, one of my favorite places in the world. Usually I met people walking their dogs, strolling with friends or running. On this day, no one appeared as I walked. About halfway through my walk was a great big tree that I had admired many times. It provided shade for the cows and horses pastured there. It was huge and graceful with a bit of character mixed in. I would talk to it once in a while because it reminded me of Grandfather Oak, but the tree didn't answer. Still, I liked to sit in its shade and rest in its presence. As I sat there, a butterfly began to dance around me. It landed on my forearm and I watched it unravel its delicate tongue as it seemed at home with me. As I sat there enjoying the butterfly's trust of me, I began to see more and more butterflies. The longer I sat there, the more I saw. Finally the butterfly flew off and I felt permission to move.

I walked out to the road and looked at the tree from a

distance. There were thousands of butterflies enjoying the sun, mating in flight and waving their wings in the wind. The tree appeared on fire as the orange monarchs took refuge in the tree. I was glad I'd taken the time to walk and that this phenomenon had been there for me to witness. I was also grateful that Mom had instilled in me a reverence for nature that continues to feed my soul.

The tree that was covered in butterflies that day.

Near Death Experience

I was seventeen when my mother died. My father was in and out of the hospital dealing with his heart condition. He was one hundred percent disabled and was unable to care for my seven-year-old brother. I tried to take care of my brother, but it was difficult to be a parent and go through the grieving process myself. My brother seemed like he hadn't grown out of the terrible two's. I had been through mononucleosis the year before and my immunity was compromised. Add the stress of my Dad being in the hospital and I was in deep trouble. We got the flu. It hit us hard.

I was caring for my brother, but was sick myself. In addition, the aspirin I was taking had expired. As I look back on that time, I see all sorts of things I could have done, but they never occurred to me at the time. I was so exhausted and sick that I went to bed and died. At least I think that is what happened.

I was looking at my body from above. I had beads of sweat on my face. I was pale and my chest no longer brought in air. Observing myself, I felt tremendous love. Like a time lapse photograph of a budding flower, life force began to return and my consciousness went back to this sweaty, sour-smelling body. A figure like Jesus came and told me I'd be all right. In that moment, I was filled with a love that cannot be expressed in words. The first time you smell lilacs or see a newborn deer, it was like that. This precious moment of being loved in every fiber of my being brought me back to life.

I read about people who are depressed and I wonder why I am not. I am grateful for this renewal of life and realized that having this experience made me feel like I had a purpose to fulfill. I feel I got a second chance.

I gathered my wits about me and it suddenly dawned on me to call for help. I called a neighbor and she got Dr. Stephens to make a house call. My brother and I got shots of penicillin and the neighbors got together and cooked meals for us. In a few weeks, we recovered. I went about my life without really examining my near-death experience. It wasn't until I began working with Jesus as a guide that I realized he had been at my bedside during that dance with death.

Synchronicity

"To walk a sacred path is to know and trust that there is guidance to help us live our lives on this planet." - Dr. Lauren Artress

By age eighteen, I had already attended one year at Boston University, my mother's alma mater. She got her wish to see me go to her college. After she died, I was free to go anywhere. I decided to establish residency in California, so I could complete college economically.

In New Hampshire, I worked with a young guy who was going back to Berkeley to return to college. He needed someone to share the drive. I had $120 and no place to stay when I got there, but I had my ride. I ended up surprising a cousin who let me stay one night, but asked me to find somewhere else after that.

Desperate to find a place to stay, I looked through the phonebook. The Berkeley Center for Human Interaction seemed to jump off the page. I called them to ask for a job. I was invited to meet with the Director to explore possibilities for work and housing. He heard my plight and offered to give me some office work and invited me stay with his family until I could make more permanent plans.

During this experience, I learned how divine guidance creates synchronicity. I spent my first night in their home getting to know the children, who were nine and eleven. I enjoyed the sense of closeness they had as a family. That evening, after the children had gone to bed, I discovered my purpose for being there. The Director's wife confided that she had terminal cancer. She said that she had been deeply moved by my family story and asked if I would help her plan how she would tell her children about her own illness.

I was able to share what my mother's dying had been like for me; how the medical processes affected me and what could have happened to make it easier to bear. This provided her with information that would help her make decisions about how she would handle things with her children, and it gave me the opportunity to heal around my own loss. It was a great opportunity to be able to support a mom in her dying process and help her know how she could handle things with her children.

His family's graciousness has encouraged me to be generous throughout my life as a tribute to them and as an expression of faith in synchronicity. I lost contact with them, but I hope they know what a great gift they gave me. I believe that there are angels in this world that show up when you need them. There certainly have been many in my life.

Telepathy Experiment

When I was in college in California, I met some great classmates. One guy was tall and lanky with wild red hair. He was nineteen and had already done the artwork on the cover of a Jesse Collin Young record album. He and I had long talks about everything. We were connected on a soul level that wasn't romance but contained a lot of love. When I decided to return to the East Coast and be with my family, we made an unusual promise to each other.

On a certain day at a specific time, several weeks after I arrived back home, I was to tune in to him and astral project into his room and he would do the same. We were to list what each of us was wearing and what our rooms looked like. I didn't think much about it until the day arrived. I thought it was kind of silly really. But I learned something on that day that stayed with me.

First we meditated at the appointed time. Then we wrote down every detail we could remember of our visions. Then we called each other and shared our impressions. I described what he was wearing and his room in full detail. He said that everything that I said was true. Then he described my outfit, my room and my mood completely. It was amazing. And an odd thing happened after that. We never spoke again. It was almost as if we had completed the mission that we had together. Or perhaps we were spooked enough to not want to connect again.

As I recall our friendship, I wonder how he is. He was one of those wonderful men who came from the heart. I wonder if he was able to keep that sweetness and creativity that were so much a part of him. Maybe somehow my book will fall into his hands and he will be warmed by the thought that our connection mattered to me.

Monks' Voices

One day, my dear friend Macy had a toe that was terribly painful and nothing she did seemed to help. I really wanted to help her. So I had her lie on her bed and did some energy healing. After about 45 minutes her energy still seemed blocked and she reported the pain was lighter but still there.

Then I got the intuition that she needed toning. Toning is using your voice to create a vibration that would break up the blockage and help things move. It is very powerful and I often wonder why many people don't understand how important toning is as a healing tool.

The trouble was that the tone she needed was far lower than my voice could go. I tried getting there and developed a scratchy throat from the effort. So I asked for angelic assistance. I asked the Monks to come and do their marvelous overtones to help her toe heal. Suddenly my voice changed octaves and I was singing like the monks in Tibet — deep resonant sounds that vibrated through the room and cleared the energy beautifully.

Macy was in a state of bliss and decided to keep resting. I went outside and sat on the grass. I marveled at the experience and spent the next moments in gratitude for the divine assistance I'd received. There will be more stories of the healing power of sound. I have been truly fortunate to work with some very gifted souls.

Surprise in a Jail Cell

"Whatever you can do, or dream you can do, begin it. Boldness has genius, power and magic in it." — Goethe

Fifty of us were standing in Liberty Park in Nashua, New Hampshire. We created a huge circle holding hands, preparing for a demonstration. Macy led our meditation. She was in her late 60s, a veteran peacemaker and the leader of our peace group. She was the kind of woman who had earned her wrinkles, and we loved her for this. She was an ex-Catholic and she didn't talk about spirituality much, but she lived her life based on faith and hard work. I admired her.

When she led us in a meditation, I wasn't expecting it to be elaborate or spectacular. But something special happened in that moment that will light my days forever.

As I began to focus on her words, the traffic noise disappeared. I felt each hand that I held grow warmer and more relaxed. She instructed us to locate the tiny spark of the divine that lived in each of us. Then she had us expand it to fortify our hearts, our bodies, and the group. Breathing deeply, we expanded the light to surround the protest site, the town, linking all nations, the planets and out into the infinite universe.

I'd done exercises like this before and intellectually appreciated the idea of unity they represented. This time though, my body experienced it. I felt infinite, connected and full of divine light. As I looked into the eyes of the others, I saw a peace that permeated their beings. I knew that they had been moved too.

After the meditation, we quietly divided up our duties. Some would leaflet Saunders Associates (where they made parts of the Patriot Missiles). Others would lead the singing of peace songs.

My group of 13 women prepared for civil disobedience. Our supplies consisted of water jugs and bright colored yarns and ribbons. We all wore our favorite T-shirts announcing our preference that the military hold bake sales to raise war funds instead of our schools to fund education, or that peace was patriotic, too.

After the leafleting and singing, we thirteen women would block the entrance to the building they called INEWS. This was an anachronism for Integrated Electronic Warfare Systems.

I had protested and blockaded before in New York City where the police officers respectfully dragged us into buses and tried to get us to tell them our real names instead of names like Sojourner Truth or Harriet Tubman. After an hour or so, they would smile and release us, telling us to stay out of trouble. One beautiful black officer, who seemed like the kind of guy you'd want for a brother, opened his jacket to reveal his collection of peace buttons. He'd said, "I'm with you, I just have a job to do." So I wasn't at all prepared for what happened in Nashua, New Hampshire.

After weaving the colored yarn and ribbons around our bodies and through the railings on the entrance steps, we proceeded to sing some of the most beautiful peace songs. We had great voices together and I confess to melting whenever I hear great harmony. We were still glowing from the meditation and the sisterhood we'd developed during our trainings in non-violence.

By the time the police arrived with their paddy wagon, we had encountered only a few employees who had wanted to enter the building. Frankly, they just went around to the back and entered there. But we were making our point, we hoped. The police wanted us to walk into the paddy wagon, but we explained that we wanted to stay. We tried to make it clear that we weren't trying to make trouble; we just wanted people to know that we did not approve of the weapons of mass destruction. We asked them to wait until the press came and got our statements before they arrested us.

What happened next took me a long time to process. Apparently Nashua Police didn't have any experience with civil disobedience and their behavior was appalling. They were quite cruel in the way they dragged us and pulled us by our hair. Their faces had turned to stone in order not to feel. I found myself wishing for the seasoned New York City cops who kept their humanity while doing their jobs. The plastic handcuffs they used tore my flesh and when I asked to have them loosened just a little an officer grabbed them and tightened them.

By the time we were all loaded and transported to the station, my hands were swollen and cold. I could feel my pulse trying to push through to my fingers. Even through this, I had a peace in my soul that kept me calm and serene. I forced myself to remember that this was the anniversary of the bombing of Hiroshima and the strength of my purpose kept me going.

The woman beside me tripped as we were boarding the elevator and the officer kicked her into it. We asked him why he was so angry. He said he didn't know and then went into a tirade about being a veteran and giving his all to his country. He said that we were a bunch of ingrates who didn't know how good we had it. We softly spoke testimonies as to why we were doing this. I told him about the pain my Dad suffered in the war and that I did this to spare anyone else from that kind of horror. I told him how afraid I was about the use of long-distance bombs where soldiers didn't see the faces of the human beings that they killed. We told him that we didn't have the answers, but that our resources needed to go toward new solutions. We explained it was our job to keep asking for that in a peaceful way. He didn't say anything, but his shoulders relaxed, and when I reminded him about my bleeding wrists, he removed my handcuffs.

We had reached the floor where we'd be booked and we were herded into cells to await our turn to be processed. This was also different than I had pictured. I thought we'd be in one big cell, like in the movies. There was a big cell, but when I asked why we were kept separate, the officer said, "To reduce the threat." I guess that's when I realized how afraid they all were. I confess to a mixture of feelings about that. I admit I felt a rush of power. But mostly I felt misunderstood. After all, we were just simple folk trying to make a point. They probably wanted to charge us with treason and hang us. That hurt. Sorrow crept into my bones as I longed for more people to understand what we were saying. I felt with all my heart that I was obligated to speak my truth even if the consequences were harsh. To expel the sorrow, I remembered the meditation. I sang the songs softly to myself and thanked the ones who had spoken before me and paved the way.

I was summoned from my reverie to be photographed. They stood us side by side and took picture after picture. They changed cameras; they changed photographers and then gruffly sent me back to my cell. As this process happened with each woman, an atmosphere of panic set in. The officers looked stiff and worried. I pleaded with one officer, who seemed to be remaining calm, to tell me what was going on. He was young and handsome and under other circumstances we might have had a date together.

He asked me, "Are you WITCHES?" I waited for a snicker or a smile that would indicate he was joking but none came.

I was in my "appreciation for the power of women" phase, so I smiled and said, "We're women," as if that would explain something. Then I asked him what was upsetting everyone.

He told me that in all the pictures the officers were showing up and the women were big ovals of light.

I said, "No way, show me." He held up a photo with a serious looking officer standing beside an oval of light.

He whispered conspiratorially, "How'd you do that?" My eyes went big and I shook my head and said, "I don't know."

Someone must have called him, because he hollered back, "Okay," and left. I never saw him again. But we shared something that I bet neither one of us will ever forget.

The arraignment was as odd as the photographs. The administration had moved a large desk into the police garage. We were herded in there like sheep and lined up about twenty feet in front of the desk. It was cold in there and we were all barefoot and without jackets. One woman was in her underwear because they had ripped her pants as they were trying to carry her to the patty wagon. The judge walked in as we were asking the officers to let us have our clothes, medicine and glasses. They shook their heads no and backed away to give the judge full attention. He banged his gavel and we were told to be quiet. We told the judge we would not cooperate until we were moved to a courtroom with full disclosure to the public. We said we had a right to our attorney, who was waiting outside for us. And we reiterated that we needed our things. He banged the gavel again and shouted that he would arraign us right here and that as far as he was concerned we had no rights. He was furious.

He began to ask each one of us for our name and addresses. Each of us gave names of famous woman. Mine was Amelia

Earhart. Each of us requested access to legal counsel, our shoes, pants, medicine and eyeglasses.

He became more agitated. He pounded the gavel several more times and then got up on the desk and screamed at us.

I became aware of the acoustics in the garage and, in a need to stay calm and dispel fear, I began to hum. As I hummed I felt my courage return. I began singing out loud, "You can't kill the Spirit, she is like a mountain, old and strong, she goes on and on…" One by one we began to sing in unison and turned our backs on the judge. He stared in amazement for a moment, got off the desk and left mumbling under his breath about having his way at the trial.

The trial became a forum for testimony about bombs and the devastation that they cause. We testified that we were not willing to continue genocide in our name. We wore T-shirts that read, "Not in Our Name". We carried that famous picture of the child running after the bomb had singed her clothes off. It was determined that we were criminal trespassers and would go to jail for ten days. I was shocked at the harshness of the sentence and sat in numb sorrow that our good intentions had been so severely punished.

I was unable to serve my sentence when the other women went. My Dad was hospitalized with another massive heart attack and in the ICU. They allowed me to serve my sentence when Dad was taken out of critical condition. I didn't think about the photographs until much later. I'm surprised now that I just put it out of my mind for several months, but I guess I was living day to day like most of us do in stressful times.

My time in jail was uneventful and I was let out in six days for good behavior. I wrote several poems while imprisoned and learned that I never wanted to be incarcerated again. I also came to believe that I no longer wanted to be against anything. I wanted to be for something and present things in that way. So now I teach the Dances of Universal Peace and use that meditation to begin each circle. Sometimes if I feel the group might be receptive, I share this experience. And anytime someone is disheartened, I know I have a story I can tell that will help give that person hope. It's one of those experiences you pull out of your memory pocket to look at once in a while when you've got the blues.

INEWS arrest photo.

Dad's Death and the Moth

I was living with my friends when my father died. He and his second wife lived a few towns away in White River Junction, where I had grown up. I had known something was coming, but I didn't know what. The strangest thing had been happening and my mind had puzzled over it for days.

I had a curtain for a bedroom door. It was a temporary situation, so it worked just fine. But for three days now there was a moth with a wingspan of at least four inches that had been holding vigil on the curtain/door. I would go in and out and tell it to go outside, but it didn't budge. I would gingerly try to pry it off so I could carry it outside, but it held so tightly that I couldn't get it off without damaging it. Periodically I would touch it to see if it was still alive because I felt it was so odd to have it stay there on the moving curtain.

I began to feel it was a messenger from the Shamanic world because the behavior was so different from other wild creatures. But why was it there for me? I certainly wasn't picking up the point of its presence. I felt sadness and couldn't explain why. Throughout the day as I worked and played I was haunted by this creature that seemed determined to stick by me no matter what.

Then I got the call. It was not a total surprise because we all knew Dad was living on borrowed time after his near-death experience, but also after nine years of having him around we took him a bit for granted. His heart gave out again and he was in a locked bathroom, so it was not easy to rescue him. By the time his wife got in to see why he'd been in there so long, it was too late. That is what Dad wanted anyway. He had not wanted any heroic measures taken to keep him around any longer. He was ready to move on.

I am primarily Kinesthetic, so that means movement and energy are most important to me. Visual and Auditory things are important too, but under stress, my Kinesthetic nature keeps me in balance. So before I went to be with family, I went for a run in the fields behind the house until I was so exhausted I couldn't move. Then I lay and watched the clouds pass by as my lungs returned to their regular rhythm. I prayed that Dad would have a peaceful passage to the true home of his soul and that he would have everything there that he needed to heal his Spirit. I cried for the loss of my Daddy and the fact that without a parent, there was no elder to guide me.

With the peacefulness that comes from nature, and having had a good cry and a good run, I returned home to dress for the family gathering. I passed through the curtain to my room and as I dressed it hit me. The moth that had held vigil on my door for days was gone. I looked around the house and there was no moth to be found. It had disappeared as mysteriously as it had come. At that moment, I knew it had been an otherworldly messenger and had left when its message had been received.

Since then I have researched the phenomenon of animals/creatures serving as silent witnesses to major transitions, especially death. I felt that it had prepared me in some subconscious way, and I sent gratitude to it for its service to me.

This experience left me with many questions. I have learned to live with questions, because I surely cannot dictate how or when the answers will come. Do these things happen to me because I am a sensitive? Do they happen because I believe in a benevolent guidance? Do they happen because I am by nature a Shaman? Do they happen to everyone, and I'm only one of a few who notices?

I imagine that there are coincidences, synchronicities and signs of loving guidance everywhere, everyday, and we would be wise to notice. Would addictions and fears be released if we knew we were loved and guided? Would we be kinder as a people if we knew there was a force watching over us? Not the punishing God of some Christian doctrines, but a benevolent force that supports us? Even if I am wrong about the existence of a Unity Consciousness that guides us, my belief in it makes me happy and many of my experiences cannot be explained any other way.

Meeting Oceania

Follow your intuition. There may be treasures there.

My car drove itself to the pet shop. I sat for a moment thinking I can't go in there. I lived in a cooperative household and I was concerned that they wouldn't want me to have a pet. In the past, I had gone to visit the animals and come away with an aching heart. I wanted a cat so much, but my life just wasn't ideal for owning one. But I had a feeling that I had better go in; some impulses are best honored.

As I walked through the door, the cat cages were on the left. From one of the cages waved a paw beckoning me over with the same gesture a person makes when they signal "come here." I was compelled to obey. This cat was beautiful. She was pure white with blue eyes. Her fur was pristine and she had a meow like a Siamese. She purred and rubbed against the cage. I opened the cage and she leapt onto my shoulder, nuzzled my neck and purred in my ear. I was hooked. This cat poured out love like a kitchen faucet pours out water.

A man came over and watched us together. He had tears in his eyes. In a choked-up voice he said he would be so happy if she didn't spend another minute in that cage. He was in the process of dropping her off and he said she was the greatest cat, and she had obviously chosen me to take her home. I was overwhelmed. I had gotten to the pet shop at the exact moment that this cat was being dropped off.

He went on to tell me that she was the offspring of one of his brothers' cats. His brother had moved to England and decided to leave them in America. That left him with the original five and two kittens. The white cat was six months old because it had taken him this long to be ready to let her go. She was litter and outdoor trained. She had a sweet demeanor and would be a fine friend.

During our conversation, this kitty quietly nestled on my shoulder with her whiskers rubbing my cheek, marking her territory. I was completely taken with her. I called my housemates and asked their permission. Not all of them were home, so I was advised to wait until I could talk to them all. So she did have to spend time in the cage, but just overnight. With my housemates' permission, I picked her up the next day.

My brother came to visit one day. I had a room with bunk beds and he was talking to me from the top bunk while I put laundry away. Someone had let Oceania inside and she came up to the bedroom. She stopped in the doorway, looked at my brother, chirped and jumped to the top bunk. She went over to his face and rubbed against it purring. My brother said, "Geez, she acts like she knows me". It was then that I realized that she must be the reincarnation of my former cat Cinders. She and I had been very close. The universe has a sense of humor, Cinders had been pure black with yellow eyes and Oceania was pure white.

Oceania was a good friend for sixteen years. My housemates shared with me that she would arrive at the door long before my car could be seen or heard. She'd sit and wait for me to arrive. When I began seeing clients at home a few years later, she proved to be quite a healer. She would get up on the massage table and curl up on the spot that needed attention. Clients would comment about the healing of her purr. It would vibrate right through the energy that was stuck in their bodies.

Toward the end of her life, she would sit like Buddha with a peaceful loving expression that always made me feel that way, too.

Oceania

New Mexico Experience

At one time, I lived in a cooperative household with six other women. We lived together to create an economical home and a sense of family. Cade and I were friends and we shared a love of nature and adventure. She and I decided to take a vacation together in New Mexico. We flew into Albuquerque a few days before Christmas. The flight was uneventful, though we were filled with wonder at the contrast of the desert terrain from our Vermont landscape. We saw the reddish brown of the soil and the green of the evergreens. Looking down, we could almost smell the sagebrush.

We were on a low budget and had reservations at a youth hostel. We would travel from there to explore. Valuing spontaneity and synchronicity, we followed clues throughout the day as to where we would go.

We spent our first day getting oriented, renting a car and gathering information about local events of interest. On our second day, we decided to go to a traditional Native American dance that happened each year just before Christmas. We stood outside the circle watching the dancers with their brightly colored ceremonial dress. The dancers began slightly out of sync, but soon their movements and the rhythm of the drums were one.

As I watched, I felt myself slip into an altered state. I began to lose myself in the beats of the drums and the current surroundings disappeared. Flashes of another scene began to emerge in my awareness as if I was watching a movie.

I watched as white men were hitting a Native American Indian. His arms were tied at the wrists and stretched out like the arms of Christ on the cross. Next, I began to feel the sting of the stick as it hit chest, face and ribs. I realized that I was this person and I was supposed to denounce my beliefs and become Christian. I also knew that I was the son of the Chief and if I surrendered, the whole tribe would. I also felt that this thing they called Christianity could not be good if it allowed this kind of behavior in these men.

The torture went on until I bled to death. I then went into the time after death where we do a review of our choices. I connected the stress of this man's death to my chronic pain in my current body. As I experienced this review, I realized that the hatred that was in me at the time of death had created this pain syndrome in my current life. When I asked a guide that was there in the review what choice he/I could have made that would have saved me from this lingering pain, I was told forgiveness. I struggled with feelings of sorrow and disenchantment. How could this victim be further victimized? How could he be expected to forgive those who tortured him? How could I?

This experience ended when I collapsed, crying beside Cade. She sat on the grass and put her arms around me and whispered that it was all right. I was safe. She rocked me and kept whispering, "You're safe now, you're safe now..." After a few moments, I began to realize where I was and we got up and moved out of the crowd. I imagine the people around us thought I had fainted. No one seemed concerned after Cade began to take care of me.

(It took me years to sort out my thoughts and feelings about this experience. I came to believe in past lives and the therapeutic value of working with them. I came to understand that I was not just a victim. I have had lifetimes of being the rigid one who tried to bend others to my will. A few months later I had a waking dream in which my husband had thrown me across the room onto a stone hearth where I died with a broken back. I was unable to clear this issue until I also remembered a lifetime as a batterer. Then the cycle was complete and the low back trouble that had been a life-long issue eased considerably.)

The next day, I was still reeling from this past life recall, but wanted to enjoy my vacation. I had Cade drive, so I could sort out my thoughts enough to package them up and put them aside until later. On our way to Taos, I asked Cade to pull over. The red dirt made me cry. I went out onto the land and began rubbing it on my body. It was a feeling like coming home. I got my water bottle and made mud and we laughed as we painted ourselves with this red earth. As the mud sunk into my pores, I felt it absorb the trauma of the previous night and begin to clear it. Who knows where therapy may come from? It certainly comes for me in the form of nature most of the time.

We found ourselves in Dixon at a restaurant called El Quinto Sol. We enjoyed the authentic Mexican food and began to connect with the locals. Dinner evolved into drinking beer and playing pool with some very handsome men.

The flirting ended when we discovered that they were married. Those married men left and one man remained. He was a fireman and told us about a cave that was unusual enough to get our attention. An artist named Ra had carved the cave into the mountaintop. We stayed at the fire station that night and the fireman brought us hiking the next morning, planning to visit the cave.

On the way up the mountain, we huffed and puffed, not accustomed to the climb or the air at this altitude. A man carrying a twenty-pound bag of birdseed jogged past us. It turned out to be the artist Ra himself. Our timing was excellent and we enjoyed chatting with him about his creation. Ra had created a mountain top cave with windows in the four directions. He carved the body of a snake at each room entrance. The open-mouthed snakehead was the fireplace. It was magnificent.

At the top of the mountain, we met a woman who would become our traveling companion for a day. Tracy brought a fun dynamic to the vacation. She wanted to go to a Buddhist Center that had a hot spring that was open to the public. We didn't find this place until late in the evening. It was a full moon. The mist from the hot spring made the night appear magical as light from the moon refracted off the water in the air. Our clothes were off in seconds and we merged into the water gratefully, as our hike and the previous nights drinking had greatly stressed our muscles.

We spent the next three hours swimming in this gloriously healing liquid. The bright moon illuminated the mountain peaks crowned with fresh snow. The next moment's image was so beautiful; it has remained in my memory to this day. As Tracy floated on her back, her round full breasts emerged with water drops glowing with moonlight. These peaks were linked with the mountain peaks and this image became linked with the divine feminine. Natural, beautiful, flowing, illuminated, sensuous and graceful — a sense of wellbeing came to me through this sight.

Tracy came back with us to Albuquerque to catch her flight scheduled for that evening. She got off just in time because when we arrived at the airport we heard news of a great storm coming. The next day was Christmas and with snow coming, Cade and I decided to stay at the hostel and rest and explore things within walking distance. We bought some groceries and settled in for the storm.

While we had been away, several people had come to the

hostel. People surrounded us from a variety of countries. People from Germany, Japan, Ireland, Brazil, Spain, Australia, Sweden, France, England, Canada and more were gathered together. Soon we were snowed in with ten inches of snow and more on the way.

The people who ran the hostel were great folks and they decided to have a Christmas dinner for us all. We each were given a task to do to contribute to the feast. I scrubbed and peeled a bag full of potatoes for the dinner. Cade was busy baking pies and biscuits. By the time our feast was prepared, we were ready to sit and enjoy our meal. As food and wine were passed around the table a sensation of great gratitude began to fill me. My ears filled with at least twelve different languages and I began to feel we were sitting down to a gathering of a global family. There was a moment of impromptu silence, which communicated to me that everyone felt this sacred connection. Then the din of many voices and many languages began again.

After dinner, we tried a game of charades. It was too complicated to organize with people speaking so many languages, so we settled for miming the movement of animals and guessing what they were by making their sounds. The evening was filled with laughter and camaraderie.

As I reflected on this, I wondered about the simple connections we make in life. Do most people, whether on vacation or in their day-to-day life, have moments where they pause and feel connected? I wonder...

Earthworks Meditation with Poppy

I went to a workshop on tuning in to nature. I was curious to learn what other people did to connect with nature and thought it would be good to be with like-minded people. We began by meditating in the building and experiencing the earth energies in our bodies. Then we were given an assignment. We were to go out and choose a flower and tune in to it. We were to receive any communication it had to offer.

I chose a huge red poppy. It was a beautiful summer day, and I was able to sit in the grass and commune with this amazing beauty. I just breathed and sat and stared at it with soft focus. I asked that it communicate anything that it wanted me to know. It was a process of focusing and not allowing anyone to distract me from my little poppy study.

As I was able to let go of distractions and fully experience the poppy, I began to feel immense joy. It seeped into my body and, like that first sip of a good cognac, infused me with warmth. I stayed there and allowed this sensation to fill me. I didn't want to go, but the warm wash of sunset reminded me that the workshop was ending and I needed to gather my things.

As I walked to my car I noticed blissful looks on the people passing by. Everyone seemed peaceful and happy. I made a mental note to meditate with flowers more often. Years later, I made a Poppy Essence that gives people a little kick of joy when they need it.

Pegasus Card from Chris's Grandmother

I fell in love with a Montana man who was spiritual and sweet and good. He was also developmentally delayed and not completely functional, but he was full of love. I tried to overlook the day-to-day details he kept forgetting, but in the end I didn't succeed.

One of my attempts to help him function was to ask my power animal Pegasus to assist him. He was sensitive, and I felt that perhaps he would benefit from her support.

On his birthday his family gathered to celebrate. His grandmother was an accomplished artist and had painted his card. It was Pegasus! As she gave him the card, she said she didn't know why she chose this image, but it just came through in the painting. Only I knew why! His grandmother was more intuitive than she was probably aware.

Grey Wolf

The Merriam-Webster Dictionary defines a shaman as a priest who uses magic to cure the sick, divine the hidden and control events. I'm certainly not able to control events. But I do see the hidden and I can help to facilitate healing. Sometimes I have to read about other people's experiences so I can realize what kind of help I need. I read Michael Harners book *The Way of the Shaman*. I also really liked Sandra Ingermans' book *Soul Retrieval: Mending the Fragmented Self*.

Sandra explains that people rarely feel whole. Because we do not feel whole, we fill ourselves up with other things – addictions, co-dependent relationships, workaholism, and even chronic illness. They may also hop from one therapy to another in search of the ultimate spiritual high.

In shamanic terms, our experience of not feeling whole is literal: parts of our soul may have split off from us and gone to other realms. This happens in order to allow the person to survive trauma or loss. Once these soul parts are gone, people may suffer physical, psychological or spiritual loss of power. This power loss can prevent people from leading healthy, creative fulfilling lives.

Ever since there have been humans, there have been shamans. All over the world, shamans have worked with people to return lost parts of their souls so that vitality and well being are restored. To do this, a shaman journeys into non-ordinary reality, searches out the cause of the trauma, and retrieves the lost parts. These ancient methods of soul retrieval are part of a body of knowledge called core shamanism which anthropologist Michael Harner has gleaned from over thirty years of cross-cultural study of native healing techniques.

Before I learned to manage my skills I felt completely

overwhelmed. Once, by accident, my awareness popped into someone's bedroom while they were making love. That was very weird for me. I was hearing voices in my head, feeling what other people were feeling, smelling illnesses and more. It was not fun. I knew if I went to the average ordinary psychiatrist, I would not have been happy with the results. So, in the early 1980's, I consulted a Shaman to help me work out the issues that I had with my psychic abilities.

This appointment did not meet my expectations. Frankly, I think I overwhelmed him. I'm not sure he had the gifts that I had. But he gave me one piece of sound advice: to always do my work through a Spirit Guide so that I am not impacted by the sensory information that comes my way. That was an important lesson. To this day I am grateful for his assistance.

After he left, I lay on my bed and did a journey to discover my Spirit Guide. It often amazes me how easily things come when I ask. It also amazes me that I often don't know what questions to ask. During this inner journey, I hunted for the spirit that would help me with my Shamanic work. A Native American arrived on horseback. He smiled down on me and said, "I've waited a long time for you to acknowledge me. You can call me Grey Wolf."

I said that I was sorry and that I welcomed him into my life. I asked him to help me work with all these confusing energies and he nodded his consent. I asked him what I needed to do and he instructed me to invite him into my day every morning as I wake up. He said that he cannot help unless he is invited. I agreed to do this, and hope blossomed in my heart.

Next he suggested that I invite a power animal to come and help me. I asked him what that is and he explained that it is a spirit in non-ordinary reality that will lend its wisdom and strength when needed. He told me that I will work with many power animals and spirit guides in my lifetime. I thanked him for his assistance and continued on my inner journey to find this animal ally.

As I continued, a beautiful white horse appeared, its front hooves dancing in the air. She whinnied and I realized that there was a horn on her forehead. She's a unicorn! I asked her how she can help me and she came close, rubbing against my spirit body. She said, "Hop on!" In non-ordinary reality you can think something and it happens, so I appeared on her back and she took me on a tour of the Shamanic realm. I saw the Cave of the Lost Children (a place where disassociated parts of us get trapped until we consciously go back and retrieve them), some of my other power animals, a place where my Spirit can rest and other places. She looked back at me and telepathically told me she represents pure love and innocence. There is no monster that can't be managed using those qualities.

Since then this unicorn is my constant guide. When we travel non-ordinary reality, my unicorn often sprouts wings and becomes Pegasus. I decided to look up Pegasus and learned that she came out of the severed head of Medusa in mythology. Medusa represents our shadow self. When we expose our shadow self to the light, beauty comes out of it. In this case, beauty came out in the form of Pegasus. I could relate to this myth because I help people cope with and learn to manage their shadows. Of course that is part of my own soul work, too.

It has been at least twenty-seven years since I first began working with Grey Wolf and my power animals. They have been loyal and loving friends. They will go with me to battle people's most horrendous fears. It is a great thing to have buddies that will literally go through hell with you. Let me clarify that, I don't believe there is literally a hell, but I do believe that people can experience all kinds of hell inside themselves.

A part of me still questions my Shamanic experiences. Even though it has been effective countless times, I have this inner scientist that really wants proof. For that reason, I went to another Shaman to have him test me. We journeyed together and when we were done, he said I was a fine quality Shaman and to trust my gifts. Through the years there have been other interesting validations of my shamanic abilities.

One special man came to me for help. He knew he had lots of potential, but he kept feeling inadequate and lost. He had a wonderful family and a great career and he felt that his self-esteem didn't match his life. I was happy to help. Through muscle testing, we determined that soul retrieval was necessary, so I prepared him for the journey. I told him that my breathing would become erratic and that I would stay connected physically by having my hand on his arm during the journey. His job was to stay awake and pay attention to what he experienced.

Over the years I had become familiar with the Cave of the Lost Children. It is a place in nonordinary reality where children's spirits become trapped. It is dense and cold, and my first time there I almost succumbed to the terrible inertia there. My power animal saved me that time, and after that I always brought help along so I could stay safe. His missing spirit child part was not there. I had to scan the earth and found a grave where his baby self was buried. I dug with my hands and brought out this corpse. There was no visible life force left. I had never encountered this before and I was concerned that I wouldn't be able to help this man.

I was inspired to call on my tiger ally and the tiger licked the baby clean with his amazing tongue. I began to see color come into the baby's face. Still that wasn't enough, but it gave me hope. When I am in my Shamanic body, I represent the cosmic mother. I often breastfeed babies back to health. I brought this spirit baby to my breast, but he wasn't alive enough to feed. I held him to my body to warm him and called on Christ and Archangel Michael to come and assist. Archangel Michael uses a blue laser beam to clear away everything that is not pure and true. He scanned through the baby several times and the child began to wake up. Christ stood vigil with me and prayed as Michael did his clearing work.

Now the baby was ready to nurse. So I held him to my breast and he fed while I soothed his fears away with my soft singing. Still this child was not fully revived. So I called on his power animal to come forth to help me and an Eagle appeared. This made all the difference; suddenly this child came alive and we were able to bring him home to his earthly body.

I believe that most of the work we do happens after the journey when I share the experience and the person reflects on the meaning for them. I always ask about their experience first, so I know it is not influenced by what I share.

My client hesitated to share his experience. He said that he was embarrassed and didn't know what to make of what had happened. I assured him that I would help him interpret it without judgment and that I knew strange things happened in the shamanic realm. He reluctantly confessed that he'd had a powerful urge to touch my breasts and that it had been very difficult for him to feel that. He said he felt depressed until an Eagle came and soared in his vision; then he knew everything would be all right.

I assured him that his vision had been accurate and his attraction to my breasts was fitting, given that as the cosmic mother I had been breast-feeding him. I also shared that until his power animal, the Eagle, arrived I had not been certain I could help him. I was happy that he was able to share this with me because it was one of the first times that a client had been able to directly experience the journey along with me. I told him that I was grateful for this confirmation.

I taught him how to care for his newly restored baby part and he went on his way. Later sessions were less dramatic, but we brought back two other parts that needed to return. He reported feeling more at home within himself. He felt stronger and more self-assured. His wife reported that there had been tremendous growth and she was truly grateful.

Another experience with Grey Wolf gave me more affirmation. I was working with a very talented man who had lost some of his self-esteem by going through a tough divorce. He was suffering greatly, but he had some important things to accomplish. One thing he was going to do was to take the talking stick tradition to an organization that needed help in their communications. They were in Wales and he had always wanted to visit there. He was enthusiastic about his mission but felt afraid that his depression would get in the way of him doing a good job.

I coached him through his reservations and fears. I decided to send Grey Wolf to protect him while he was in Wales. He seemed to be buoyed by this idea and so it was done. During the two weeks that he was away, I had all sorts of problems. I was out of sorts and void of the synchronicities to which I had become accustomed. I came to learn that lending out your Spirit Guide isn't a great idea for the lender.

He returned from his trip with a good report. He said the events had gone well, his travels had been great and an amazing thing had happened. He handed me a portrait and said, "Does he look familiar?"

I said, "Why yes, that is Grey Wolf."

He told me how the portrait had come to be. A student in his group was an artist. She had walked up to him at the end of the day and apologized for staring at him so much during the workshop. She explained that there had been a Native American spirit standing beside him the whole time. She had drawn him and would he like the portrait?

He was flabbergasted. He thanked her for this great gift and looked forward to sharing the story with me. I still have a copy of the portrait and when I need the strength and reassurance that Grey Wolf embodies, I can look at it. What a lovely confirmation! And I was very grateful to have Grey Wolf back!

Grey Wolf

Road to Claudia's

A large part of my profession is based on training from Three In One Concepts. It teaches kinesiology, which is muscle testing, and provides hundreds of corrections that restore balance to body, mind and spirit. Muscle testing gives the practitioner access to a client's own deep body wisdom where unconscious programming can be revealed and corrected. I learned to love its effectiveness and efficiency from receiving treatments from Claudia. Claudia started me on a healing path that was a part of my soul purpose.

However, I didn't know that right away. All I knew was that some friends liked her and that she was a two-hour drive away and that the treatments cost half of my meager weekly salary. So I was on my way to this appointment, but my mind was thinking that I was crazy. I was having the guilty inner dialogue I had every time I spent money that I didn't really have to spare. I was driving myself crazy with what meditation teachers call the "monkey mind." I was so exasperated by my self-doubt that I yelled out, "God, show me a sign that I'm on the right track!"

Claudia does Stress Diffusion sessions and channels a being called McDermott. I had signed up for the whole nine yards figuring it would make the long drive worth it. So when, within a few minutes after asking for help, a truck with the sign McDermott Trucking passed me on the highway, I began to relax. But slowly my doubt took over as it often does with just one sign, so I asked for another. A few moments later, a truck went by with the huge letters G.O.D. on its sides. So I followed my fate. I'm glad I did. Claudia helped me to know my true self and modeled a healing process that would become my primary healing modality.

Kinesiology from Three in One Concepts is a marvelous tool

to support a client in discovering the source of their stress with an issue and relieving it so that their divine intelligence can shine through.

Rainbow Smiley at the A-Frame

It's a good idea to ask for signs when you are questioning your choices: interesting answers come. I had just moved into a little A-Frame that was still being renovated. It had plastic for some windows, and the former tenants had left a mess. It was, however, in my price range and it was kind of cute. Still, after two solid days of cleaning I became discouraged. What was I doing here? I didn't know anyone in the area, the house felt isolated and the leftover energy from the last folks was not good. Back then I didn't know how to clear houses, so I was feeling stuck. Once again, I yelled out to the divine "Help, I need a sign!"

Nothing came right away. Exhausted, I took my aching, tired body to bed. In the wee hours of the morning I heard a squeak. It gradually permeated my awareness and woke me up. Great, I thought, a mouse — just what I need. I turned on the lights and began searching for the creature so I could catch it and throw it out. I should have noticed that my cat was still sleeping and wasn't showing any interest, a clue that it was not a mouse that I was hearing.

I had scrubbed every inch of this place in the last two days. There was no matchbook or marble or anything that could still be lying around. Slowly I narrowed down the area from where the sound was emitting. I honed in on it and there I found a four-inch-high rainbow-covered furry stuffed animal with star antennas (picture below). As soon as I found it the squeaking stopped, and I had to laugh. This smiley, furry little creature was truly silly looking. I went to bed and decided that I had received my sign. Have a sense of humor, girl!

(I have since discovered this animal is a character from the
Rainbow Bright children's program.)

Grandfather Oak

In the early 1990s, I had the privilege of becoming a caretaker of a beautiful estate in Cornish, New Hampshire. I lived in the guest cottage and took care of the place. The owners were away most of the time, so I had the place to myself. There were gardens that were over one hundred years old. Monkshood, antique roses, lady slippers, lilies and peonies adorned the perimeter of the lawn.

Standing vigil for at least two centuries were four oak trees. I came to love this little backyard paradise. The oaks protected me and I would sit at their base on soft moss, feeling safe and loved.

One day in my second year there, I heard in my head the stern voice of the oldest oak. He said, "You may call me Grandfather."

I dismissed it as my imagination, as I often do with these psychic experiences.

He repeated with vehemence, "You may call me Grandfather."

I began to accept this communication and replied, "Thank you, Grandfather, for your communication. What would you like me to know?"

"I will teach you many things, but the most important one is to trust what I say."

"This is not normal communication and it takes some getting used to, but I will work on it," I replied.

"Here is your assignment."

Oh great, I thought, I have work to do.

Grandfather Oak obviously heard my thought and said that I would enjoy the work. It was what I had come here to do.

Another thought escaped while I still carried the illusion of privacy. "You mean mowing the lawn, weeding the gardens and raking the leaves isn't enough?"

All connection stopped. The warmth and protection I had

come to take for granted had gone. I was no longer connected to this beautiful being.

In an arrogant reaction, I said "Fine!" and went inside.

A few days later, I realized that I missed the Oak's great presence. The magic was gone. So, I went out and said I was sorry to have been so rude, and could we start again? Suddenly I was filled with the connection again and I heard. "Welcome back. You are most certainly stubborn, but we will start again."

And so we began a relationship that was full of magic and wonder and love. I would invite people over and test their awareness. Often they would say they felt this was a special place, but they never mentioned hearing Grandfather Oak talk to them.

One week Grandfather told me I would make essences that Friday. I was to make Mallow essence in particular. I told Grandfather that would be impossible because I had a full day with clients and I knew there was no Mallow on the property. He said, "Wait and see." For the rest of the week I searched for local sources of it, but no friends had it and what I saw in my travels was in strangers' yards. So I let go of the idea that I would be creating a Mallow essence.

When Friday came, I went out to the Oak and said that I couldn't do the assignment because I had clients and no Mallow. Just then the phone rang and one by one my clients canceled their appointments. I made some disparaging remark about the guides and angels having no regard for someone's need to make a living. As I stewed about my finances, I walked around the gardens smelling the flowers and picking out weeds. As I came to one garden I saw a small bush full of pink flowers. It was a mallow in full bloom. This was my second year as caretaker there. It had not been there the day before or the weeks before or even the year before. I knew every inch of the gardens.

So I made Mallow Essence and Grandfather certainly expanded my sense of what was possible. I wish I could say I never doubted again, but doubt is just part of who I am. But grandfather and I had a good relationship and when I get a chance, I go back to say hello and honor the tree that taught me to trust that the miracles happen.

I am hugging Grandfather Oak

Montana, Dakota and Mariposa Lily

I was invited to go stay on a beautiful ranch in Montana that was owned by the family of a dear friend of mine. They hosted me to work with friends and family doing private healing sessions. I saw twenty people and worked with some animals, too. Some pretty amazing sessions happened. It was a time of openhearted healing, and people took leaps in their growth that made it very fulfilling.

What happened in my free time really stands out in my memory. It was April, sunny and incredibly beautiful. The mountains still had snow, but the land showed fresh new spring grass sprinkled with field flowers. I love horses and was given the opportunity to ride a faithful trail horse named Dakota. I was a bit rusty on riding, so they gave me the reliable, stable horse. I was grateful for the security I felt riding Dakota. He seemed to know what I wanted before I did. I didn't have to kick him to trot or pull back on the reins to slow down. He just knew what I wanted.

After a week of rides, I was really in awe of his ability to "read" me and serve me in such a sweet way. We explored the ranch that went on for miles and I was in heaven. I usually rode with a group that was checking fences or herding some of the cattle or just out for the joy of the ride. But after they saw that I was safe with Dakota they gave me a chance to go out by myself. I had no idea what was in store for me.

As I traveled alone this day, Dakota seemed like a different horse. He was not following my directions at all, let alone reading my mind. He was downright obnoxious. I was having a miserable time and considered going back, but it was such a gorgeous bright sunny day and I had worked so hard the day before. I really wanted to explore. Then a thought occurred to me. Maybe I should just let him take me where he wanted to go.

After about forty-five minutes, we crested a hill and down the entire side was a field of Mariposa Lilies. These elegant white flowers filled the air with their sweetness. The sun poured over the flowers and made them glow. The energy there was amazing. I got down off Dakota and immersed myself in the beauty. He had taken me there on purpose. It was the reason he hadn't followed my directions. There was something so sweet about being taken care of by this dear horse. What amazing magic!

Dakota and I returned the next day and I meditated with the Mariposa Lilies and made an essence from them. For the next two years, muscle testing revealed that most clients needed Mariposa Lily essence to heal issues with the divine feminine. I remembered allowing Dakota to lead me, thus allowing the divine feminine to work through him. And because I allowed the divine feminine to guide the process, I received a generous gift!

Ranch in Montana

Animal Healings

After a client develops trust in the kinesiology process, they often ask me to work with their pets. Just as human care consists of more than a doctor can offer, pet care takes more than a veterinarian can offer. A lot of what I do is determining why an injury isn't healing well or a behavior isn't resolving. The other major piece is helping the human caretaker to decide when to assist in the dying process and when to simply let the dying process continue. It is a relief for people to know they can ask their pets' bodies, with muscle testing, what is going on. Then the people know they aren't just guessing at what their pet needs. Here are some experiences that stand out as extraordinary.

On a ranch out West, three pregnant mares were being rescued from the glue factory. This ranch is a wonderful place that spends 7 days/24 hours a day closely handling the newborn colts and fillies. This teaches them to trust humans and eliminates the need to "break" them. They care for their animals really well and these horses were very lucky to have been rescued. But they didn't act it. They were jumpy, and the first birth did not go well.

The birth was difficult and both mare and colt were weak. I was called in to see if I could tell what was going on because they should have been thriving. I was surprised to see how nervous they were when I approached because horses usually take to me right away. I chose to tune in to all the mares at once to see if there was a common issue. There was. Horses think in pictures and that is how we can talk to them, by sending pictures.

Unfortunately everyone working with these poor horses kept remembering that they were originally going to the glue factory, so every day the horses received this old picture. They didn't know they would live their lives out on this beautiful ranch in utter comfort. So I sent a picture of them on the ranch happy and healthy. I embellished it with eating lots of grass and hay, drinking water and running around in the pasture. I also pictured the old idea fading away and the new plan getting brighter and stronger.

The next part was to get everyone who worked with these horses to completely switch what they pictured. They were instructed to do the fade of the old program and to adopt the new program of living a happy life on the ranch. They were instructed to make it bright and full of detail. A few days later the next colt was born with ease, and both mare and baby were happy and healthy. The third mare was the same. Now they all live in comfort, no longer nervous that this was a temporary stop on the way to destruction.

Your thoughts have a huge impact on your pets' behavior. If you keep picturing their misbehavior, you will perpetuate it. They are intuitive creatures, so your words are only part of the communication; what you envision is also a big part of what they read from you. The innocent act of worrying can mean the difference between a pet getting well or not. It is perhaps a great lesson for us regarding the complexities of communication.

This is also true of children. I have watched parents make sure their children's negative behaviors will linger by labeling them, worrying and picturing the bad things they do, or by only responding to the negative so the child has to act up to get attention. We can have a positive impact on all of life if we learn to recognize our thoughts and how they affect others.

I heard an interview with Ram Doss when he had just been officially declared a master in a spiritual tradition. When asked how he was different he said, "I still have the same negative thoughts, I just don't entertain them as long." (I'm quoting from a radio interview that I heard so it is a summary of the idea, not necessarily the exact text.) But my point is that even a master has negative thoughts, so don't judge yourself for having them, just let them go sooner. I found great solace in his words because I couldn't stop having negative thoughts completely, but I had absolute choice about how long I let them run in my mind.

Meditation training is a good way to become successful at managing your thoughts. *The Course in Miracles* is another way to understand how much our thoughts influence our experiences. I am grateful to have both of those disciplines in my background as they have helped me in all of my work with animals, children and adults. And certainly the quality of my life is better when I discipline my thoughts. I no longer wish to have anger at someone who drives poorly, or takes a long time in the checkout line or gives me less than perfect service. Sometimes I counter those experiences by being an exceptionally courteous driver, an efficient customer at the store, and I try to do something to enhance a service persons' day. Try being a "good fairy" for a day and sprinkle every interaction with kindness and appreciation of others. You will have a wonderful day. It really works.

A friend of mine feels he has to teach a lesson to every discourteous driver on the road. He gets afraid and angry at everyone who tailgates, cuts him off or doesn't dim his lights at night. I do not enjoy riding with him. If I'm driving, he criticizes me. The entire trip is miserable. I've watched him get more and more shut down and dysfunctional when driving. It recreates trauma every time he goes out. It makes me sad. At some point we have to take responsibility for our fearful thoughts and let them go. Once I said to him that instead of focusing on all his driving issues he could be noting the beautiful trees, feeling the freedom of traveling, noticing the sunshine or grooving to the music. He said, "That's your job." But underneath his sarcasm he knows it's his job. I'm going to keep picturing traveling with ease, pleasant conversation, humor and beauty.

Let's get back to the animal stories. There was a beautiful racehorse that had injured his knee and could not race anymore. A client of mine had adopted him, and he was causing all sorts of trouble with her other horses. His knee was not healing, either, and the vet had done all he could about it. So she called me in to muscle test and find out what his body, mind and spirit had to say.

When I tuned in I got a picture that he was still revving up for the races. That was why he was agitated and not relaxed around the other horses. So the first thing I did was fadeout the picture of him racing and replace it with a picture of him living harmoniously on the farm. I also made sure to include him enjoying the other horses. Then I muscle tested what his knee needed. It turned out there was a nutritional deficiency that was easy to remedy. So within a week, this great horse became calmer and friendlier to the other horses, and his knee was healing well. We also gave him Rescue Remedy, a Bach Flower Remedy that releases trauma, in his water. It worked like a charm.

On another occasion, I was called to help Posey, an elderly cat that wasn't feeling well. She was grieving the loss of her cat buddy, Copper, and would stare out into space as though she was seeing something. She wasn't eating much, and she just seemed to be fading away. I was able to see that Coppers spirit was still hanging around. I asked permission to send him on to the light. First, I had to reassure him that Posey would be all right without him. Then he moved on his merry way. Within a few days Posey began eating again and perked up to be her usual self.

Posey's owners were intuitive, too, and they heard her ask to have that nice lady come over again. So they invited me to dinner and Posey sat with me and licked my hand, telling me she was grateful for the healing. It was sweet.

There was a beautiful golden lab, Truly, who was riddled with cancerous tumors. She was fairly young and her owner wanted me to help her decide what Truly needed to heal. I got the impression that the tumors were willing to leave if the owner would deal with the emotions of a difficult divorce. How do I say that to her? So I just asked if she had something emotional going on in her life that was really upsetting her. She told me about the divorce and how painful it was. Here was a case where the dog brought the human to me for treatment. The person became the client and over time Truly's tumors disappeared.

Dogs can be very devoted. They are also energetically sensitive. If you aren't dealing with something traumatic, your dog could very well be picking it up. Do yourself and the dog a favor by getting the help that you need. This applies to cats and horses, and birds to a lesser degree. It is really the service-oriented dog that picks up human issues the most.

Ranch in Montana

Bird Assignment

When you are an Earth Steward as I am, you get some weird assignments. And it's not as though someone tells you what those assignments are to be. Things just show up for you to deal with and you end up learning as you go.

Birds showed up in all sorts of health. Most came to die. Some came to heal. It started when I lived in the A-Frame on Stage Road in Plainfield, New Hampshire and to my surprise it continued when I moved to live on St. Gaudens Road in Cornish, New Hampshire. I never did figure out how I got to be the caretaker of these distressed birds, but they somehow knew to find me.

It all started with a flicker who hit the house. When I checked to see if it was stunned or dead, I discovered its neck was broken. I felt the life force leaking out of it and said a prayer. I decided to bury it in the yard, so I left it in a Kleenex box on the deck. I dug the hole and said goodbye to this delicate creature. Then I became fascinated with its feathers and little body. With utmost reverence I explored every little detail. The delicate beauty that I could see up close enthralled me. Did you know their breast has a group of white feathers with a black heart shape on each one? I felt this was a gift and I saved a few to go into my medicine pouch.

Then a few weeks later I found a dead hawk in my yard. I guessed that while in flight it had been hit by a car. I was able to hold this magnificent being. I meditated with it for a few moments because hawk is one of my power animals and once again I felt blessed, though uneasy about this pattern that seemed to be developing.

A chickadee, two blue jays, a robin and a grosbeak appeared and were buried. I was getting quite disturbed by this strange series of events. Each time I did a prayer asking that their soul go on to their next highest level of vibration. Each time I dug a hole and buried them. At this point I was deeply concerned. What message had I sent out to the universe that caused this response?

I never got the answer to that question. But when I began having the same experiences in my new place I decided to protest. Holding a beautiful, dead grouse in my hands, lifting it to the sky, I shouted, "No more birds, I don't want to be a midwife to these dying birds". Then I said the usual prayer and buried the grouse. It never happened again.

As time went by, I was able to enjoy living birds in their proper place. I began to relax. Perhaps some guide or angel had heard my plea and had released me from that assignment. To this day I wonder.

Service Call

Two days before Christmas, I received a call from a job agency to fill in for Carol, a caregiver. She wanted time off to be with her family. The woman that I was to care for was very ill and that scared me, so I said, "No" right away. Then I thought about it. I intuitively knew to call back and say I would do it. I was single and didn't have children. I could give this gift of time off to someone who probably worked very hard and most likely had a family hoping to spend the time with her. So I called back and got the address and instructions for my upcoming adventure. I sure didn't know what I was in for!

The agency that had hired me explained that she was not going to be a fun person. She was an alcoholic and she was reputed to get angry a lot. I meditated before going over. I asked my guides and angels to help me support her and make this a special day. I felt a sense of peace, knowing however bad it was, it would only be for one day and at least I had my spiritual team to help me.

I found the house and knocked on the door. A lovely gentleman let me in and thanked me for coming. He explained that his wife was dying. She had cirrhosis of the liver and was not eating or drinking. He said that she hadn't slept in weeks. He apologized for her in advance and said that she was irritable and difficult. He said that she wouldn't like me, but that I shouldn't take it personally if she yelled or called me names. It was just the way she was now that she was so sick. He explained that he had to work, but would be back around six p.m.

We went into her room together and he introduced us. She seemed to accept the change in personnel without a care and I was grateful for that. I admit I was scared when I saw her. She was frail and thin and there were bruises all over her body. I was instructed to take her to the bathroom if she asked and help her in any way she needed me. I was left with the husband's phone number and this stranger in my care.

She spoke very little. Her throat was dry, so she practically barked out her orders. She used two or three words at a time, never really speaking a whole sentence. Much of my time was spent trying to understand what she wanted me to do. She said things like "stand now" or "bathroom." In an effort to stay awake, she had me help her off the bed every fifteen minutes or so. I agonized over doing this, because every time I touched her she developed another bruise. Still, I followed her wishes and walked her around the room or into the bathroom whenever she asked.

A television was on, which she seemed to use to stay awake but didn't really pay attention to. As she stared at the TV images, I went into another meditation, asking the angels to ease her pain and help her understand what she was going through. This was about six hours into my eight-hour experience. I was discouraged and saddened by her condition and my inability to relieve her suffering. What was I doing there? I had settled into believing that my service was indeed to her usual caregiver and not necessarily to her. Then she suddenly spoke.

"You have six things to teach me," she said, startling me out of my meditation.

"I'm sorry, what did you say?" I said, my spine tingling with anticipation.

"You have six things to teach me," she repeated adamantly.

My mind searched for what she might be referring to and I realized she needed to learn what I knew about the dying process. Suddenly my purpose in being there became clear and I took a deep breath. I organized my thoughts, realized I didn't know if I had six things exactly, but I'd share what I knew. I told her about my Dad's near-death experience and my own. I shared with her the studies by Dr. Raymond Moody about the dying process. I talked about Elizabeth Kubler Ross' five stages of dying.

I told her that I had prayed to the angels to help her in her transition and that I was confident that they would be there for her. Anticipating that she may have some remorse about her behaviors as an alcoholic, I told her that it doesn't matter how we have been in our lifetime, for at the moment of death, all is forgiven. She was quiet for the full forty-five minutes while I spoke. When I was finished she nodded and went to sleep.

I finished off my time with her by scanning her sleeping body intuitively and sending Reiki to the areas that needed it. I watched the angels beam healing rays of light throughout her body. She slept soundly.

When her husband came home and found her peacefully sleeping, his eyes filled with tears and he said, "How did you do that? She hasn't slept in weeks. She looks so peaceful."

I told him about my meditations, our talk about death and the Reiki healings. He gently took my hand and kissed it. He looked into my eyes and said, "You are an angel. You have given my family the best gift we could receive this Christmas."

I hugged him and thanked him for this opportunity. I told him that I hadn't been able to be this present for my Mom when she died and it was healing for me to have been able to step up and be there for his wife. His son was arriving as I left, and I felt good to have served this family.

It could have ended there, but it didn't. I carried her in my heart for the next few days. I prayed for her continual healing and gentle passage. On New Year's Eve, I meditated on what I wanted for the New Year. I let go of unforgiving places in me and wiped the slate clean. In my meditation, she came to me. She was flying and waving. She had a big grin on her face. She thanked me and said that I was right about it all. She was free. A few days later, I looked for her obituary and there it was. She had died on New Year's Eve.

Fire Walk

I have a strange relationship with fear. I don't respect it much. I have this sense that if I just see through it, I'll discover the message behind it. I think many fears are based on false assumptions, and that if we were honest with ourselves, we'd discover the limiting thought behind each fear. Many people think all fear is real and make choices based on it. Not me. I suppose that makes me a good life coach. I pass on my determination to discern the limiting thought behind the fear, so that my clients learn to do that too.

But sometimes I miss the good information fear could teach me. Sometimes it keeps you in balance to acknowledge the fear and speak to it respectfully. But don't ever let it bully you around, because it's usually just old patterns coming to be healed. For instance, pain can be reduced dramatically when you reduce the fear of pain. It is often the fear of pain that is much worse than the pain itself. The next time you get a pain, watch what your mind does with it. It will amaze you. It will take off and run a dozen scenarios about it. Thoughts of cancer and other diseases may begin to creep into your mind as though they were real. It will teach you a lot about pain to follow your fear of it.

I remember reading the book *Mutant Message Down Under.* I don't care if there was a controversy about its authenticity; I learned a very important truth. When the natives sang the song of wholeness to the broken leg, reminding it that it knew how to be whole again, it made sense to me. After studying Deepok Chopra's quantum physics and how our bodies renew themselves every few years, I realize we have healing potentials that we are barely using.

I am a Reiki Master and know that Reiki can remind our bodies of our perfect balance. I had an experience that verified the validity behind the song of wholeness. While I was a caretaker in the beautiful Cornish estate, their rental house down the road was getting a new roof. I was supposed to check on the progress periodically and report to the owners in Florida. One day I went there while everyone was out for lunch. I walked around outside, looking at things. Suddenly my leg went into a large hole that had been covered by a tarp. I heard it snap and I knew it was a bad sprain. I sat down right where I was and called on the Reiki energy and sang a little song to my ankle of its wholeness. I sang about the blood vessels flowing easily, the tendons and muscles feeling ease and comfort and the bones being straight and strong. And to my relief, I walked out of there with only a slight tenderness.

Now remember, I am not prone to exaggeration. I heard and felt a snap in that ankle. It had the potential to be a very serious sprain or even a break. But it wasn't, and I believe wholeheartedly, that was because I took the time to remind it that it could rearrange itself back into wholeness.

After that, I felt different about myself. I felt that I was a participant in my own healing in a more empowered way. I was not a victim of circumstance and could make very healthy choices simply by changing my attitude.

Later, I was able to test this in some interesting ways. I was a mentor for the daughter of some dear friends. As a way of thanking me, she invited me to her family's celebration party of her high school graduation, which was a fire walk. Her uncle conducted firewalls in Maine and came to treat us to this empowering firewalks seminar. I was excited and felt that I would be able to do it, but was very curious to learn what it would take to get us there.

I enjoyed her uncle's approach. He took our group, consisting of her classmates, friends and family to a place of relaxation and positive thinking. He told stories of amazing things people can do and gave examples from quantum physics so that we could begin to see that we were capable of miracles.

We were able to break boards and bend rebar. We were feeling really good about ourselves. We went outside and began to see the fire glowing red in the darkness. With no moon or stars to light the sky, the red of the coals made eerie images of the participants. Our faces were shaded, like we wore primitive masks.

I was feeling quite primal and powerful and excited. We stood in line and our guide gave us instructions as we prepared to cross the coals. I imagined him saying all sorts of profound things to each person and so I was surprised when it came to my turn he bent close to my ear and said simply, "You can do it." but by that time I knew I could do it. So off I went across the coals saying my mantra, "I am one with the fire. I can do this." And I did. I even went again because I have this quirky thing that doing something once isn't quite enough, I have to do it at least twice. Maybe that is the scientist in me saying it isn't accurate until you can duplicate the results.

During my second walk, a tiny bit of coal stuck to the bottom of my foot and I got a slight burn, but nothing substantial. Nothing could possibly dampen my feeling of empowerment. Some of the group did not walk. I felt badly for them because I wondered if they would question themselves about it later.

So I was feeling pretty high and had cheered all those who walked as well as for those who didn't. Our facilitator made sure that those who chose not to walk were respected for their choices and were given support for that too. It was a great experience, but it was after midnight and I was tired, so I prepared to go home.

My friend asked me if I wanted a flashlight because it was so dark. I had walked to their house and was going to walk home. I refused, saying I knew the way really well. She shook her head and said, "Okay." Well, I really should have taken that flashlight. This would have been a time when a little fear could have been useful. I should have taken some time to eat a snack and come back down to earth before I attempted to go home. In retrospect I think I was a little ungrounded.

I felt my way home with my bare feet, because it was so dark I could not see at all. My progress was slow and I considered turning back several times. After a while, I managed to feel the difference from the dirt road to the gravel driveway, so I knew I was close. Even so, inch by inch I kept going and wasn't reaching the house. It was bizarre.

Finally, I found myself trying to rush and not getting anywhere. Then I realized I had been at this for so long that I had to pee. So I just squatted right where I was. Certainly there was no one to see me and it couldn't hurt the driveway. Without that pressure to get home fast I moved a few feet and sat down. I closed my eyes and asked for help from Spirit. The answer came right away in the form of a picture. I had gotten sidetracked onto the large, rarely used circular driveway and had been going round and round in circles! I thanked Spirit and made my way to the house.

I had been lost in my own driveway. I know, it's crazy. I had just walked on fire for goodness sake. I had to laugh. I rarely get to have an inflated ego for long. I must be meant to be humble this time around, because I sure felt humbled that evening! What a contrast from walking on fire to getting lost in your very own driveway!

Sue's Dying Process

"It is extraordinary how extraordinary the ordinary person is." —
George F. Will

I met Sue in 1998 when I worked at a weeklong retreat called Wellspring at Juniper Hill Lodge in Windsor, Vermont, for people with cancer. She certainly looked ordinary: middle-aged, overweight, graying brown hair and a sprinkling of freckles. I had the privilege of giving Sue her first Reiki treatment. It gave her some relief from the pain of her lung cancer. I didn't know it then, but that would begin a long and important relationship.

As I reflect on the retreats I feel a sense of nostalgia. I want them to happen again because I saw people connecting on an intimate level that was precious. I saw the participants receive massage and energy work that gave them positive touch, which we hoped would make up for some of the pain of hospital procedures.

Sue asked me to continue Reiki treatments once she went home. I was able to meet with her every two weeks for two years while she prepared to die. I had many mixed feelings about doing this with her. I didn't know her before the retreat, and as I worked with her I realized that I was beginning to love a dying woman. Not a romantic love, but a love that comes from sharing from the deepest heart level. I was conflicted because I had lost many people I had loved and I wanted to become more carefree and joyful, not more grief-stricken. I wonder if the saying was true that God/Guidance doesn't give you what you want, but gives you what you need. Did I need more grief?

As I worked with Sue, I coached her on how to complete things with her grown children, friends and community. I was able to help her deal with her life in a way I had not been able to with my mother. That is what I came to believe was one of the purposes of my being there with her. She gave me the opportunity to heal by allowing me to recognize that I did have what it takes to support someone who is dying. Sue was funny, insightful, courageous and outrageous. She had a deep sense of the Divine Feminine. She was not able to walk comfortably into the arms of the 'Lord," but was able to see herself surrendering to the Goddess. So her struggle was ancient, archetypal and beautiful.

In the first year that we worked together, she got the overwhelming desire to plant a moon garden. So each of her friends brought her white flowers and gradually her garden grew to be a celebration of the Goddess and the moon. As the moon became full, she watched it grow brighter and brighter until it appeared to light up at night.

She became forthright and would recount stories about her challenges to doctors and nurses. As a former local nurse, she was respected and what she said seemed to sink into the psyches of her former coworkers. She would chastise them about not returning her calls within a reasonable time or about the way they danced around her dying instead of being honest. She was an advocate for all cancer patients because she was honest in her own dying process. I don't think any medical personnel who came in contact with her got away with much. She fought through the pain and the despair to be clear and represent a population who are often too sick or too disempowered to speak up for themselves. In this way, she began to see meaning in her dying.

Sue didn't go quietly into the night; she kept us all on our toes. A few months before she died, she asked me to be one of her midwives to her dying process. I knew a bit about how a midwife supports the birthing process, but what was it to support the dying process? Would the hospital respect our role or would they fight us on following her wishes? Up to this point I had been making home visits; could I stand making hospital visits? I was not happy with how hospitals did things and I certainly didn't like the sharp reminders of my experiences with my Mother's and Father's dying. Every breath I took in a hospital, with its alcohol and disinfectants, made me return to the painful memories of losing my mother and my father's times in the ICU. My fears overwhelmed me. Would I fail Sue in the end if I agreed to this? Or would I fail her even more if I refused?

I am not one to back away from challenges or responsibilities. I told her I would be there for her, but that I wanted her to know I was scared and overwhelmed by the idea. She said, "How do you think I feel?" thus putting it in perspective. That was Sue. She never let anyone get away with self-indulgence, unless one called it that and included chocolate in the process.

That February I had to move because the mansion, for which I was caretaker, was sold. I was grieving for my sanctuary. I was also in the middle of a horrible flu. I had a fever and a cough that shook me to the bone. I was exhausted and weak. The people who were buying the place saw how much distress I was in and took the last truckload of my things to my new apartment. Then the call came. Sue is in the hospital; it is time for the midwives to gather. What kind of cruel joke was this?

I wasn't able to gather my strength for the first few days that she was hospitalized. I had to rest and recuperate. Finally, after four days I was able to take my place beside the midwives Ina and Ginny. Ina is a grand goddess. She carries an intellect and presence that is regal and earthy at the same time. She and Sue shared some great moments of healing with the divine feminine. Ginny is a sweet, loving woman who was family and friend to Sue. She kept the practical things like water and guests flowing. But what was I there for?

The hospital staff was wonderful. Many of them had worked with Sue, and they respected her wishes about having us there and leaving her without too much intervention. She had her own morphine drip that she could administer for herself. She was dosing herself frequently because she was in a lot of pain. I gave her Reiki and flower essences. As I sat with her she would say, "I'm ready to go, why can't I leave?" I'd shrug my shoulders and hold her and offer her more Reiki and flower essences. The flower essence that she used the most was one called The Universe Handles the Details.

Her pleas to have me help her let go were hard for me. I felt like I was failing her. So when her doctor came in to check in on her, I spoke honestly to him. "She is ready to go, but when I see her energy try to leave it only gets halfway out to her adrenal glands and then zaps back in". He nodded his head, said he knew what to do for her and later a nurse came in with a new IV. It contained a milky liquid that the doctor later referred to as milk of amnesia. He said that it would help her body let go.

At that point, I understood my role in her process was to give her Reiki, flower essences and tell the doctor what I saw psychically so he could know what was happening. A few hours later I watched as her soul slipped out of her body and moved dreamily into the afterlife. It was a translucent representation much like her physical body, but more like light. And then she was gone. Peace filled the room and I knew her journey was complete. Ina led us in an anointing ritual with essential oils, herbs and songs. We cried softly as we sang and wished her bon voyage.

Sue, you were a teacher for me. I am grateful for your courage to die consciously and for including me in that process. I am grateful for your insistence that I face my fears and serve as one of your death midwives. And I am grateful for the amazing grace that you shared with us along the way. Your stories of synchronicities and heart-to-heart conversations will live in me for the rest of my days.

Amazingly this whole process took only a few days. Then I was back in my apartment setting it up. I was surprised to find myself happy. I would miss her, but I had a sense of fulfillment and acceptance that I knew was connected to her passing. And I had a sense that I had managed a rite of passage for myself. I'd faced death in all its stages and I wasn't more wounded, I was more whole. I imagined the spirits of my Mother and Father rejoicing in my growth and being glad that I had found freedom from old regrets.

"Be at peace with your own soul, then heaven and earth will be at peace with you. Enter eagerly into the treasure house that is within you, you will see the things that are in heaven; for there is but one single entry to both. The ladder that leads to the Kingdom is hidden within your soul. Dive into yourself, and in your soul you will discover the stairs by which to ascend."

— Saint Isaac of Nineveh

Sound Healing

I was planning to attend a workshop on the healing power of sound that was presented by Steven Camp. I knew intuitively that I would love this training and I was excited about going. As the time came to get ready to go, I found more and more reasons to stay home. I developed a great fatigue and a sense of despair began to overwhelm me. This confused me. I was spiritually guided to go to this workshop and yet, I felt physically inhibited to get moving.

I had just read a book about parenting your inner child. It suddenly occurred to me that maybe a part of me didn't want to go. So I took out paper and a pen and wrote out this dialogue.

I am excited about going to this sound-healing workshop. Why do I suddenly feel so tired?

No answer.

I am going to this workshop!

No!!!!!!!!!!!!!!!

Okay, who doesn't want to go?

In my mind I see a five-year-old pouting, so I say. What is the matter? Why are you sad?

If you make me go, I'm going to scream!!!!!!!

Okay. Why don't you want to go?

Because I'm going to cry.

Why would you cry?

Because I have a lot of feelings when we work with sound.

Okay. How about if we tell everybody that we might cry and it's okay.

No then they give us attention and send sorry feelings to us and it makes us feel worse.

Okay. How about if I say we will feel feelings and ask that

nobody worry about it because some of the feelings are really good.

Maybe. (still pouting)

Well, if we don't go now, we aren't going to get there on time and I'm going to feel both mad and sad.

Okay.

So do you take away my energy when you are upset about something?

Yes.

Can we get to know each other better and stop that?

Yes.

So if I pay attention to what you need more often, I won't get tired as much?

Yes.

So we continued this dialogue for the forty-minute ride to the workshop. Most of it was fine-tuning what I would say to the group so that the little girl inside would feel protected emotionally. When I arrived, the workshop was just starting.

Steven asked each of us to share why we were there and what we hoped to get out of the workshop. I was one of the last to share and I simply said that I might cry because sound work means so much to me. And that I hoped that no one would worry about my crying because I felt it was healthy.

Steven got very excited and thanked me for saying that. He said it was very important to notice what we were feeling as we did this work and let it flow. He shared that he had seen amazing healing when people released their emotions.

I was grateful to him for appreciating my request and my inner child was too! Steven taught us how to clear the spine and chakras with sound. It was quite profound. He also led us to create harmonic overtones. I use this healing work in my private practice with almost every client at some point in his or her healing process. I am so glad I worked through the resistance and made it to the class. I have a better relationship with my inner child too.

"Only when I make room for the voice of the child within me do I feel myself to be truly genuine and creative" — Alice Miller

Vacation on Maui

I had not had a vacation in ten years. A friend suggested that we go to Maui. His intuition strongly guided him to take me there. I told him if he could get tickets for under $700.00, I would do it. I had investigated the prices and knew they were usually double that. When he came back with a price of $658.00 I knew I was meant to go.

The biggest miracle of this trip would be that it would introduce me to a place that I would later call home. And there were a few more surprises to come.

When we arrived, we were tired and sore from sixteen hours of travel, but it was manageable. In the airport, I naively expected to receive a lei. When none appeared, I asked my friend why we weren't getting flowers. He explained those were for people who came in groups or for special occasions. While we waited for luggage we began to talk with a couple who lived on Maui. They were very sweet and checked on us to make sure we got a rental car. They handed us their phone number and said they would be happy to have us visit for dinner. That was my first experience of Aloha. There would be many more.

Later that week, we called and made arrangements to have dinner with this lovely couple. When we arrived at their door, she presented me with my first lei. It was made with beautiful, deliciously fragrant white Pikake flowers. The kindness of the couple overwhelmed me. They gave us advice about where to visit and their favorite beaches. We were truly blessed by their generosity.

The road to Hana is full of cliff-side views, hairpin turns and irresponsible drivers. It is amazingly beautiful and nerve-wracking at the same time. My friend was driving. On the trip back, I began to get nauseous and asked him to pull over so I could get some air and calm my stomach. As I got out of the car, I realized that we were in alignment with a brilliantly gorgeous rainbow. Rainbows on Maui can be spectacular. They span the sky with such vivid colors; it seems you can almost taste them. I often felt that the rainbows provided healing because each chakra can be strengthened by its color.

Feeling better, I looked down from the high cliff to see what was at the end of the rainbow. Two turtles swam there. Later, after living on Maui for a while, I would realize how much I treasured turtles. I have come to think of them as an animal ally otherwise known as a "power animal." Turtles became teachers and healers for me.

We stayed at a hostel called Banana Bungalow. It was rough and certainly not in any part of Maui we wanted to explore, but it had some great points. We met people from all over the world. We had a tour guide who took us to some really beautiful sights for as little as five dollars per trip. We enjoyed sumptuous African foods cooked by one of the many fascinating guests. It was an interesting way to be initiated into the Maui culture, which is perhaps more of a "melting pot" than New York City. I relish the richness of the languages, the exotic flowers and the extraordinary smells of the rare variety of foods.

I wrote this poem at the beginning of my time on Maui.

Take away my work
Take away those who need me
Take away my car
Take away my email
Take away my phone
Take away my schedule
Take away my cats
Take away my familiar surroundings
And what do I have?
Who am I?
What new possibilities emerge?
What are my longings?
In what new ways can I express who I am?
What is underneath my habits, my roles, and my routines?
Who am I?
I followed new longings and discovered
They lead me into amazing places
Like the first time I discovered what lies
At the end of the rainbow:
There swam a turtle family.
The mama was so big I saw her
From a cliff, swimming with her babies.
Or getting tossed in the waves,
Not knowing which way was up
And being reminded how small I am in the scheme of things.
You'd think that would be scary,
But instead it was comforting.
Janet Heartson, 1998

Eventually, we found some lovely beaches. I was grateful to

immerse myself in the warm, aqua playground. Swimming in the salty ocean allowed me to float for hours. My body learned to relax more deeply than it had in years. The rhythm of the waves, the color of the sea, sky and sand, all became therapy. I floated in the thick, buoyant, salt water and breathed in the fresh air. The giggles and squeals of playing children began to teach me to release responsible adulthood and to embrace playfulness.

I didn't know that Maui was becoming a part of me or that in a few years I would learn to call her home. It was not an easy trip. There were many painful moments such as poor communication with my travel companion or uncomfortable experiences like getting seriously tossed in the ocean, but my fate was unfolding.

Here is a poem that I wrote about my trip to Maui.

Sea Grace

Floating weightless
Fish gleaming in schools
All around me.
The sea reveals itself
With such grace
All things liquid floating.
Seaweed clouds
Migrate across the bottom
Like dancing tumbleweed.
Sunlight filters down
Streams of golden delight
Illuminating all.
My mind floats too
Blissful suspension
Holy communion.

I rented snorkel gear and got the five-minute training about how to snorkel and where to go that was safe. Ulua Beach was commonly recommended because it was easy to get to and somewhat safe for tourists. While snorkeling there, I discovered a whole new world. Suddenly the colorful fish weren't limited to pictures or a tank. They performed their ballet all around, above and below me.

Out of curiosity, out of ignorance, I explored around the coral and a sea urchin placed its sharp needles deep into my hand. I deserved it. I was the trespasser. It hurt so much I began to cry.

The sting was tremendous and I learned from experienced divers the remains of the needles take time to dissolve. You just have to wait it out.

When I learned I wouldn't die; I went back into the ocean to explore again — this time far from the spiny coral. The colorful iridescent fish seemed not to ignore me but to want to perform instead. Then I heard it. At first I thought it was a child's delightful squeal, but no- it was a whales' song. My heart leapt to attention as I realized that this was why I had come for the love of whales and dolphins. Or so I thought. But I learned with another kind of knowing it was for their love for me. I heard in their song, love so vast, so wise, so all encompassing, all my defenses melted. My heart was already full, and it opened even more as their song permeated my being. They are my mother, my father, my sister, and my brother. They hold my longings, my callings, my sorrow and my joy.

Songs Inside My Head

When I first arrived
The verse that repeated itself
Over and over inside me was
"Where do I go to find familiar?"
I knew it was a reflection
Of how lost I felt,
Surrounded by newness,
A different language,
Different and powerful terrain,
Oceans and cliff sides.

Then after some deep crying
And the graciousness of time
Another verse emerged.
"I have a million nightingales
On the branches of my heart"
Flowed through my mind
And sang itself throughout my day.
I knew I'd made the transition
And rediscovered my joy.
And soon the Hawaiian language
Became a song that sang
Itself into my heart.
The pound of the surf
Mingled with my own rhythms
And the cooing of the doves
Became my familiar wake-up call.
I find myself back home in New England
But I believe that Mother Maui

Has initiated me in some way.
Somehow knowing her has changed me.
Hearing the whales' song
Has stretched my heart beyond recognition.
They've told me of a secret unity
That will never be lost
For it now lives within me.
I accept this sacred blessing.

One Hundred Percent Love

"Every aspect of our lives is, in a sense, a vote for the kind of world we want to live in." — Frances Moore Lappe'

I recycle everything, even other people's trash. I helped my neighbors move, and in the process I discovered that they didn't feel they had the time to recycle. I made a mental note to go through their garbage and sort out the glass and plastic and paper that could be put to good use. Okay, I know that is a bit excessive, but it only took me an hour and I felt really great about doing my small piece on Mother Earth's behalf. And I got a bonus that I never could have anticipated....

In the garbage, I found a cool vase, a magazine I was interested in and an old video of some guru. I was curious about the video, but tucked it away for another time.

I have suffered from insomnia for at least 20 years and I've learned to get up and read or watch a video or listen to a meditation tape. So when I couldn't sleep I just got up and turned the TV on. There was nothing I considered worth watching at 3am, so I dug out that video that I had rescued from my neighbor's trash. It was boring at first, but I was glad for that because I thought it might help me get sleepy.

As this woman is describing her experience of Sai Baba, I watched the room suddenly light up. Everything became energy that glowed and I became aware that everything is living and vibrating, even the furniture. I had only previously experienced this in a very high group meditation, so I sat up and took notice. Putting my skepticism aside, I said out loud, "Okay, if you exist and would like to help me I am open to your healing." As they say, be careful what you ask for.

After a few minutes, I began to feel sleepy and I gratefully returned to my bed and drifted off. In my dream state what happened next seemed perfectly normal, but when I awakened I was quite amazed.

Sai Baba came to me in my sleep and asked me "How much love do you want?"

I replied, "Twenty percent."

Sai Baba looked forlorn. He shook his head and asked, "Wouldn't you like more than that?"

I realized my mistake and said, "How about eighty percent?"

He gave me a look of such compassion and sadness, and then he zapped me with one hundred percent love.

What a lesson I received from this Master. How could I not ask for one hundred percent? I really had to look at the way I measured my self-worth and my concept of how much I deserved to receive. He was a good friend to come to my dreams and heal me.

So if you get an urge to recycle someone else's garbage, be aware that there may be prizes there.

Bees

Bees have always fascinated me. The Montshire Museum in Norwich, Vermont, near where I grew up, had a bee exhibit. I loved to watch them work together for a common purpose. I guess I wanted what they had, a community where the individual is important, but the unity is always more important. Some museum visitors would express discomfort, fear or disgust when they looked at the exhibit. I just felt love. I've had some amazing experiences with bees.

In the early 1990s, I lived in a sweet little cottage in Norwich. Part of my rent was doing things for the owner such as mowing her lawn when she went away. I didn't mind mowing if I could use a self-propelled mower and there weren't too many steep hills. With Fibromyalgia, I realized I could get things done like mowing, if I rested well afterwards. However I had been in a lot of pain in recent months, so I was afraid it was going to deplete my energy. But as you may have learned, people who have Fibromyalgia tend to be very responsible and try hard to do everything they commit to doing even if they don't feel well.

I always say a prayer that all creatures get out of the way before I mow because once I hurt a frog while mowing and I was devastated. The mowing went smoothly this time. It was a beautiful day and other than my runny nose from my allergy to the new mown grass, I was enjoying the process.

Suddenly I felt a sting in my right buttocks. I reached behind and brushed a bee off. I must have disturbed him. The sting hurt quite a bit, but when you have chronic pain, you get used to working through it. So I finished the lawn and went inside for a cool glass of lemonade. I make it from fresh lemons and sweeten it with honey. I thought about the gift of the honey possibly from the very same bee that stung me. I decided that I was more grateful than angry. Little did I know just how grateful I'd be.

That night I was able to get a lot done. I felt energy and a fluidity in my body that I rarely felt. The next day, the sciatica that is always with me in my right buttock area was gone. All that pain had been lifted. Then I noticed that nothing hurt. None of my twenty something trigger points were hurting. It was surely a miracle.

That bee had given me a reprieve from constant pain and I was glad to be alive! What an incredible gift.

Now fast-forward to Maui in 2002. I have a little cottage in Kula, a beautiful upcountry space. Part of my rent was to mow the lawn, weed the gardens and take care of the grounds. I've been lucky to find rentals that were reasonably priced because there was some work involved. I would have done the gardening for pleasure, so it was great that it helped with the rent.

The rose-scented geranium grew in huge clusters and filled the air with its rosy, lemony scent. A wise person has rose geranium wherever they live, because it lifts the spirits and helps maintain vitality. The clover was abundant, too. This was not the ordinary clover of New England. These grew huge and purple and unbelievably sweet. I was conflicted about mowing it down so I picked bouquets of it and left them on friends' doorsteps.

Later in the week there was a cloud of bees hovering over my garden. I stood in awe as they vibrated there. As they migrated toward the house, I backed away and went off to work. When I came home, a hive had settled in my front bush. Rosemary grows as big as lilacs from New England and they were happily buzzing around one of the larger branches. They must have been attracted to the tiny purple blossoms on the rosemary bush.

I often look for meaning behind an animal sighting or an encounter with nature that seems personal to me. I thought about bees being a symbol of fertility and I connected viewing them to my grieving as I processed the fact that I could no longer consider having children. In my late 40's with no partner in sight, I was beginning to realize that I needed to let go of the idea of being a mother. Though the rational side of me had decided that I would not have children due to overpopulation and my particularly poor genetics, there was a part of me that just didn't want to let go of having that option. Were the bees there to assure me of my fertility or were they simply enjoying the clover, geranium and rosemary? Was this a message or something simpler?

I was having a tough time with my health. I had a job that required me to work about fifty hours to get paid for forty. With my health issues, forty hours was all I could manage, so this was really taking its toll. Added to that was the fact that I was working with drug addicts who neglected or abused their children. I was given the daunting task of training them to be good parents. It is very difficult to parent a child when you are focused on getting your next fix. So my job was next to impossible. This is very draining on the soul. Had I had it my way, the parents would have gone to rehab to clear the drugs out before I had to work with them on the fine art of parenting.

During a session with teenagers who were having a tough time with their domineering father, I fell on a gravel driveway. My knees and left arm were bloody from the dive into gravel. My ankle was sprained and my hands were bloody and bruised from trying to catch myself while falling. I also knew that I had not tripped to cause the fall. My legs had just given out beneath me. This was very scary.

So, later that week I had a MRI to investigate why my legs were giving out from under me. I was flown to Oahu where they had the tests called evoked responses and the MRI machine. I was scared and alone in this process. After a very long day of flying and medical tests, I was grateful to come home. My cat Ipu greeted me at the door and seemed particularly affectionate. I made supper and sat down with my legs up on the couch. I sat enjoying the vibration of her purr on my legs and then realized there was a second vibration. I put my ear to the wall and heard the most amazing buzz. When I touched the wall with my hand it was warm.

Remembering the bees from earlier that week, I checked the bush outside. There were no bees out there. They had worked their way into my wall and picked the spot that would be beside my right ear when I sat on my couch. I knew this had meaning for me, but I didn't discover it until later that week.

My neurologist had the tests back and we met so I could hear the results. It was clear that I had MS. Multiple Sclerosis. He recommended a drug and he wanted to do a spinal tap to measure something in the fluid. Well, I always think of medical tests in this way: if I were to have the results of the test, would it alter my treatment or my behavior?

Since having researched MS as my possible issue, I knew that the consensus was the drug made you sick two days out of seven, so I opted out. Having decided that the neurologists didn't have much to offer MS patients, I looked into alternative treatments. There was one that popped right off my computer screen: bee sting therapy!

That's what the bees were there to tell me. We are here for you, Beloved. We offer our support in your time of need. We want you to know you have options. As I opened to their messages, I felt warm loving feelings and most important, I was reminded that the divine in all its manifestations was there for me. I am loved.

Rosemary bush where the bees made their home.

Pink Lightning

When you ask for something that you want and your heart is open, it is likely that the universe will do its best to give it to you. I was coming back to New England from Maui and I was longing to see deer, lilacs, fireflies and seagulls. I was raised around all of them and, in addition to friends and family, they were what I longed to see. I had also been reminiscing about a time when my mother and I had sat outside under a blanket in a thunder and lightning storm. The lightning was pink. I still have the sky-blue blanket that we used as our makeshift tent.

As I gathered my things and my wits about me to prepare to depart the plane and begin my vacation, I saw a flash. As I watched for another one I mused at how neat it would be if it were pink. I sent a message to the spirit of my Mom that I would be amazed if she orchestrated pink lightening for the beginning of my trip in New England. Just then another flash confirmed it. I was watching pink lightening. As the oo's and ah's began to fill the plane, I sent a silent thank you to those divine beings that love to give us treats. So I made note to watch for other ways this vacation would reveal itself as special.

My friend Gavin picked me up at the Boston Airport and we were catching up on each other's lives. We went to stay in York, Maine, at my friend Donna's house. The next morning, while making coffee, I looked out her kitchen window and there in her yard were three deer. I marveled at their beauty and realized that I was being given another gift. I went outside to see them and they stayed for a few minutes until I tried to pat them and they ran back to the woods. Then the scent of lilacs wafted through the air. I put my hand on my heart in gratitude. As if that wasn't enough, seagulls flew by announcing their presence with their typical laughing. I began to feel that some intense magic was afoot and that I was the lucky recipient.

Now one could argue that the things I longed to see were typical in New England and so these events were hardly special. Or were they? The very first night I saw pink lightning. The first day I saw deer, lilacs and seagulls and that evening while we watched a concert in the park, fireflies danced. I said a prayer of gratitude before I went to sleep that night for special friends and nature's incredible gifts.

As the vacation progressed, blessings appeared everywhere in many forms. I will share the most outstanding ones. I went to my nephew's wedding and had a very good time. It was relaxed and fun, and I got to see people whom I cherished all in one place. When it came time for the bride to toss the bouquet, I remained seated chatting with my sister Kathy and laughing at the antics of my dear great niece Molly. The DJ paged me to come up to try my hand at catching the bouquet and I shook my head and continued our conversation.

Well, this DJ didn't let up. I was paged several times and the whole group was waiting, so I finally conceded and took my place in the back of the group. I knew my brother had orchestrated this embarrassing moment, so I was busy scowling at him when the bouquet practically jumped into my hands. A wild cheer filled the wedding tent and there I stood with the flowers.

Now, I am considered the hippy of the family. I wore Birkenstocks and ate tofu long before it became commonplace. I also haven't always been much of a girly girl. I don't paint my nails or toes. I cut my own hair and frankly I don't shave my legs every day. So when my brother, sister and niece all asked me if I'd shaved my legs, I figured they were just teasing me. My answer was a slightly irritated "Yes". In unison they asked, "Recently"? What on earth was causing them to ask these personal questions? Then it dawned on me that catching the bouquet wasn't the end of this rather silly ritual.

And then I saw that this gorgeous boy who must have been all of 21 was holding a garter and signaling that I should sit in a chair in the middle of the circle. This boy who could be my son was going to place a garter on my leg, and I would let him if I were truly a good sport. So down I sat with my cheeks a shade of thoroughly embarrassed pink, and he placed this lovely lacy blue item on my thigh. Poor guy. He was so gracious or disappointed that he didn't even look while doing it. Where do these traditions come from? I chalked this up to giving me a funny story to tell and walked away hoping that people had better things to think about than this embarrassing moment. Of course I was wrong. My marital status or lack thereof was immediately the talk of the afternoon and I heard many speculations that I would finally find the love of my life because I had caught this damned bouquet. Okay, I admit it. I was glad when it was time to go home and my personal life was no longer the subject on everyone's mind.

As odd as it sounds, the ritual did make me wonder. Was I going to meet the love of my life? Two weeks before I left for my vacation, an astrologer had told me that I was going to take a trip to the past in a few weeks and meet my mate. She said don't worry you don't have to think about it, you'll meet him with a grocery cart or something simple like that. And you'll know. I passed this off as someone telling you what you want to hear and let it go.

At the end of the vacation, I went back to my friend Donna's house with another friend Robyn. Donna and I have been single a long time and we love each other. We jokingly said that if we were eighty and still not married, we'd get together. Since it is nearly impossible to change your sexual orientation, we didn't plan on that really happening. Robyn is happily married, but she listened as we joked about the woes of being single. We laughed a lot that night and said goodbye to Robyn who had to leave early that next morning.

The next evening Donna and I were cooking dinner and listening to a CD. I stopped chopping and turned to Donna and said, "Who is this singing? His voice sounds like home." Donna gasped and said, "Oh my God, you have to meet him! I met him through a dating service and we weren't right for each other, but you two would be great together!" His name is John Heartson and we were listening to his CD: Beyond the Stars. She called him and left a message inviting him to breakfast the next morning.

Well, his cell phone had gone to messages because he was about to go grocery shopping in Price Chopper (remember the reference to a shopping cart in the astrological reading). Later that night, he called and said he'd be glad to come to breakfast. It was a two-hour drive from his home to Donna's. He joked and said, "Well, I love breakfast." But I know he was guided to meet me that day. We felt at home with each other right away and have since become life partners. I moved back to New England to live with him. The astrologer, Kimla Dodds was right and maybe catching the bouquet really did have something to do with finding my true love.

Saying Goodbye to the Ocean

Sometimes we make decisions that we are meant to make but that doesn't stop us from hurting. Having fallen in love with a man living in New England, I needed to leave my beloved Maui. But spending five years in such a beautiful place changes you. Maui lives inside me now and like severing a toe, it hurt to leave her. Everywhere I walked I winced because I was already missing Mother Maui's grace. Every moment of the last few months was bittersweet. My excitement to play out this new love was mixed with grief.

Aloha is everything. It is hello, goodbye and love. That says it all. What else is there? Even now as I look back on this time, my eyes water and my heart aches for the smell of mock orange, jasmine and gardenia. Here in New England's stark winter with the colorless outdoors, I remember the vivid blue of the ocean against the white sand. I breathe in the hibiscus colors of tangerine orange, fluorescent pink and regal reds. I remember the green landscape offering itself as backdrop to the elegant blooms of wisteria, bougainvillea and passionflower. My toes ache to be barefoot in the sand. Like a footprint on the beach, I have made my impressions there. The dolphins, turtles and fish have all paid homage to me in their own ways.

I learned to snorkel soon after moving to Maui. It was my kind of sport. I was able to exercise without getting too hot. I was entertained by an amazing array of exotic shapes and colors. I was getting tan and great muscles in my arms and legs. Each time I went out, I ventured a bit further until I could swim for miles at a time.

Since receiving my dual diagnosis of Fibromyalgia and MS I had learned to give up jogging. I missed it, though. When you run, you get into a rhythm that takes you into an altered state. It has been referred to as the Zone. I loved that place and finally I'd discovered a new exercise that didn't create wear and tear on my joints. I went into the Zone all the time when I snorkeled. I would hear my breath go in and out and my heart beat in time with the movement of my arms and legs. The rhythm of breath and heart become hypnotic.

On one of my last voyages out snorkeling in the sea I was blessed to have the spinner dolphins come leaping about two hundred yards from my friends' boat. I excitedly leapt out of the boat and swam toward them, but they had already gone. They swim sleek and fast and you can't catch up with them unless they really want you to. So I sang a love song, "Won't you listen, listen, listen to my heart song, I will never forget you, I will never forsake you." I lay suspended in the water singing out my grief allowing my tears to mingle with the salt water.

After a few minutes I heard the high-pitched greetings of the dolphins. They had heard my call and had returned to circle me. Round and round they swam. Two dolphin couples of the pod of eight were making love as they wove in and out, surrounding me with their love. My giggles made bubbles through the snorkel and tickled my nose. One dolphin came even closer and we made eye contact. Once you have been eye to eye with a dolphin, you know what matters. This honest love is greater than a hundred kisses, even great kisses. It pours through you like honey dissolving in warm tea and sweetens your life. I was truly blessed.

On another goodbye snorkel, I communed with the turtles. One turtle had a tumor on its head. It was the first one I had encountered when I began going to this favorite beach. I hadn't seen him for months and I'd wondered if he had died. He greeted me and I followed him to a group that was hanging around in a beam of light by one of the coral reefs. There were all my favorite characters and I felt like a child at a surprise party. All my turtle buddies had come to say goodbye. I swam amongst them and said a silent prayer of gratitude to my first loyal turtle friend who so kindly threw such a glorious going away party.

On the way back to the beach, I was tired and satisfied with my morning's adventure. I couldn't have dreamed that there would be more. There are schools of fish called Silversides that are silver with very big eyes. They were often around the turtles, and I would come each day and sway with them in their schools. I would just float on the water breathing through my snorkel tube, literally hanging out with these fish. If I made a sudden movement they would shift away in unison. I admired their capacity to demonstrate such beauty by doing their synchronized swimming.

They must have decided to say goodbye as well. They began to circle around me. More and more fish joined in until I could not see through them or below them. I was surrounded by a tunnel of silver, which swirled more and more rapidly around me. The light filtered down into the sea and reflected off their beautiful bodies, creating a tunnel of light and sparkling eyes. As I floated there, I became mesmerized by this passionate display of attention. I cannot recall how long this experience took place. I only know that at the end, the fish gradually parted and I returned to the beach.

I couldn't speak of this for a few days. Even now, words barely brush the surface of that encounter. Inside I understood that the sea had honored me with a party of friends who somehow knew I was leaving and wanted me to know that I mattered. The love that I had poured out as I had navigated this water wonderland had been felt. Those creatures knew me and loved me.

How lucky I am to have this relationship to nature that creates reciprocity so few humans have the opportunity to experience. Nature is so abundantly generous. I need only choose to love and a world of wonder opens to me.

"The deepest secret in our heart of hearts is that we are writing because we love the world." — Natalie Goldberg

Conversation with Grief

I enjoyed Sue Monk Kidd's book *The Secret Life of Bees*, so I was excited to see that she had written another. *The Mermaid's Chair* is very powerful. I found myself getting involved with the characters and caring about what happened to them. I'm an emotional person and I have jokingly rated movies by how many Kleenex I need to get through them. Deer Hunter was a five-Kleenex movie, as was *Terms of Endearment*. By page 288 in this book I had a line of seven tissues rolled up like snowballs on the coffee table.

It was about the death of the main character's father and the pain her mother felt while retelling what had led to his death. Having lost my parents early in life, I sometimes find myself grieving vicariously through movies and books. As I struggled to see through my tears and continue reading, I felt a chill. I looked up to see the door had blown open. Well, you know by now that I believe in all sorts of things including Spirits, so I thought perhaps someone had come to see me. The logical thought was that one of my parents had come to visit. I had felt their presence before, but I intuitively knew it wasn't one of them.

I gathered my courage and asked who was there. I was told, "I am your grief."

I said, "Why have you walked in the door?"

He answered, "So you know that I can walk out again. I am here to ask you why you hold me so close. Why don't you ask me to leave?"

Pondering this, I asked myself, "Have I benefited from my relationship with grief?"

My answer was, "Having known such loss, I am more grateful than most. And I am more compassionate than many because I know suffering."

Then Grief asked me, "When is it enough? Do you need to grow more compassionate or more grateful? What will it take to say goodbye to me?"

I think, "Is it okay to do that?"

"Yes," replies Grief. "I can always come back if I'm needed."

I ask myself what will take his place. I think: graceful movement, joyful play, creativity and comfort. When I think "comfort," I realize that the Fibromyalgia and MS have some connection here.

Grief notices this line of thought and responds, "You are already a Velveteen Rabbit, well worn and well loved. How much more worn do you need to be?"

One of the common threads in both Fibromyalgia and M.S. is that the myelin sheath is worn away, exposing nerves and causing misfiring. So this line of thinking has great meaning for me.

With resolve, I get up, open the door and usher him out. Smiling to myself, I wonder what healing will take place as a result of this decision.

Here is a poem I wrote the night before this experience with my unexpected guest:

There are necessary losses.
We are meant to know hurt.
We are meant to know darkness.
We must carry the stones of our regrets,
Until we nearly drop, spent and exhausted.
Only when we can hardly move
Do we realize that letting go of each stone
One by one can make us new again.
I have carried mountains.
My body is old and worn,
But each time I let go of my burdens
I am free.
Would I know freedom had I not suffered?

Thank you, Grief, for showing up and teaching me to let go. I am free.

Your Healing Possibilities

Albert Einstein once said, "There are two ways to live your life. One is as though nothing is a miracle. The other is as though everything is a miracle."

Miracles come most often when we are open and when we are actively healing. They come when we are grateful and humble and know that we are a small but mighty piece of this world.

I have the best job in the world because I have the delight of supporting clients in removing obstacles to their own miracles. They often come back with reports of synchronicities that amaze us both.

Here are some examples of the beautiful healings that I have had the joy of facilitating.

A boy was able to stop a facial tic when he learned how to deal with the frustration of having a brother with autism.

A Mom was able to improve her relationship with her son when she discovered that he wasn't ignoring her, he was deaf.

A woman was able to enjoy swimming again when she uncovered her fear was from a time when her older brother had gotten too boisterous and made her afraid that she was drowning.

A man who had shoulder pain, discovered that it was from age 15 when his dad had died and everyone said it was his job to take care of his mother. He was shouldering the burden and that was connected to the pain of losing his father.

A woman with a debilitating fear of snakes discovers its source and now walks in the woods with ease.

A woman who was recently divorced and felt suicidal was able to cut the cords between her and her ex and she suddenly felt liberated and free.

A family who had problems after moving to a new house was

able to clear the energy and restore their happiness. The house was formerly owned by a couple who had divorced and their argumentative energy was stuck there until we did the session to release it.

A house had been on the market for years and was finally sold after we cleared it of some ghost like energies. It sold within the next few weeks. Actually, I love to clear homes to either help the current families feel happier or to help them sell. I have a near perfect success rate for getting a home sold.

None of these things would have been discovered as quickly (one session) without the use of muscle testing. It is a brilliant tool that directs all of my sessions and has never disappointed me.

My life is only beginning now that I am in my fifties. It amazes me that I feel so young and free, now more than ever. I didn't set out attached to being young, but I seem to become younger as I become more authentic. Or perhaps it's just that my ego doesn't care how old I am, just if I am "living in accord with the promptings which come from my true self".

I've always loved the image of the spiral. When I read about the Fibonacci code and the life formula within the spiral, I had a sense of my connection with all that is. To recognize creation is to be a part of it.

"The hero's journey is not a linear path but a spiral. We keep circling through its archetypal manifestations at different levels of depth, breadth and height. It is not so much that we go anywhere but that we fill out... The journey fills us out and gives us substance. People who have taken their journeys are bigger — even if their bodies are thin or they are small of stature. We feel the size of their souls." — Carol Pearson, *The Hero Within: Six Archetypes We Live By*

In *Love, Medicine and Miracles,* Bernie Siegel, M.D. wrote:

"My advice is to live your life. Allow that wonderful inner intelligence to speak through you. The blueprint for you to be your authentic self lies within you. In some mystical way the microscopic egg that grew to be you had the program for your physical, intellectual, emotional and spiritual development. Allow the development to occur to its fullest: grow and bloom. Follow your bliss and be what you want to be."

If you would like support in living to your fullest, please visit my website www.heartsons.com for information about booking an appointment.

May you come to know the miraculousness of you!

Navigating Your Own Extraordinary Moments

This section is to help you navigate the extraordinary moments that you experience. It is a set of tools that help me and my clients. If I have not given proper credit to something, it is because it was handed down to me via oral tradition and I don't know where it originally came from.

It is not easy being sensitive, but I wouldn't trade it for anything. It gives me a sense of oneness that is fulfilling to me. I hope that these exercises and tools help you.

Sometimes listening to your intuition is a life or death issue. Recently a young mother was murdered. A couple called and asked for her help because their car was broken down. Before she left, she called a friend and asked him to check on her if she wasn't back in an hour. Unfortunately she was murdered. Her intuition told her it wasn't safe and yet she was so good hearted she went anyway. Please learn to listen to your own inner wisdom and don't let your generous nature over rule it. Our community lost a wonderful teacher, a family lost their daughter and especially sad, a two year old boy lost his mother.

I have many examples of how listening to my intuition was important to me. One example is that one day I couldn't get out of my own way. Even though I value being on time, I kept prolonging my stay at home and I was getting irritated at myself. Finally, my energy freed up and I was able to leave for my appointment. I passed an accident that had just happened. I would have been in that accident if something hadn't held me back each time I tried to go out the door. So value your instincts, impulses, guidance, gut, etc and even if you don't see the big picture, trust your guidance.

Even the fact that you are reading my book is a form of guidance. You are reading it because there is information that you need and this book will affirm your inner wisdom.

ENERGY CLEARING TECHNIQUES

Why is it important to clear my energy? If you want to feel clear and respond the way you want to others, you definitely want to master your energy. Emotional Freedom is important to all of us.

Symptoms of not being clear:
1. Over reacting when someone does something that hurts your feelings or makes you uncomfortable.
2. Road Rage
3. Negative communication cycles with loved ones.
4. Tired and cranky
5. Unfocused, easily distracted.
6. Life has lost its appeal
7. Feeling like a victim
8. Not feeling like you can accomplish what you want.
9. No sense of humor.

What it feels like to have clear energy:
1. Feeling empowered to reach your goals.
2. Having the energy to make life work for you.
3. Responding with compassion and patience to those that matter to you.
4. Not taking it personally if someone else drives badly or is rude.
5. Speaking your truth and trusting that it will create a trusting relationship.
6. Joyful moments of insight.
7. Experiences of synchronicity.

Techniques to clear energy
1. Drinking Water
2. Alternate Nostril Breathing
3. Using Affirmations
4. Brain Merge
5. Color Drain
6. Frontal Occipital Holding
7. Roots
8. White Sheet
9. Column of light
10. Prayer
11. Human Car Wash of Light
12. Golden Vacuum
13. Ya Hayy, Ya Haqq

DRINK WATER!

Many physical and energetic problems are caused by dehydration and you won't even notice it. We don't get thirsty until we are down 2 quarts. That means a lot of problems can happen before we might recognize that we are thirsty.

Most people would feel a lot better if they drank 32 ounces of water each day. If you need help keeping track, fill a quart bottle and make sure it's gone by the end of the day.

ALTERNATE NOSTRIL BREATHING: This process is ancient and powerful. It is tricky to do with a cold or after crying, but sometimes your nostrils will clear if you persist in the process.

1. Use your pointer finger to block your right nostril and inhale through theleft nostril.
2. Switch and block your left nostril and exhale through the

right.

3. Inhale right nostril

4. Switch and block left nostril and exhale.

5. Inhale left nostril.

6. This is one repetition. Continue this process until you have done 10 repetitions or until you feel a sense of well being or relaxation.

USING AFFIRMATIONS: This can be helpful to change how you feel about yourself, someone else or a situation.

1. Always state something in the positive. If you are critical of your body, for example, the affirmation could be "I love my body". It doesn't matter if you don't believe it yet. You are reshaping the neurological path with a new way of thinking.

2. Say the words out loud with enthusiasm.

3. Rub your ears while repeating the phrase at least three times.

BRAIN MERGE: This is useful to access whole brain thinking and relieves stress. Our brains are more efficient, creative and strong when both sides work together.

1. Imagine that your brain is split down the center in two halves: right and left.

2. Imagine the left brain being one color

3. Imagine the right brain being a different color

4. Imagine they merge to create a totally new color. (It doesn't have to make sense like blue and yellow making green)

COLOR DRAIN: This is to support someone in clearing an emotion that is interfering with what they want to accomplish.

1. Go inward in your awareness and find out where the emotion is in your body (this works for pain and tension also).
2. Discover what color it is.
3. Feel what temperature.
4. Discover any other senses associated with it such as smell, sound, texture etc.
5. Develop a drain and let the emotion (pain, tension) drain out of your body.
6. As it leaves, allow a color that represents what your want to feel to come in.

FRONTAL OCCIPITAL HOLDING: This is useful when you are having the same old reaction to something and you want to shift your attitude.

1. Put one hand on your forehead
2. Put your other hand on the occiput behind your head as demonstrated.
3. Deep breathe thinking about how you want to shift your attitude. (I want to accept this child, I want to show compassion even though this person is irritating to me, I want to be patient while standing in this line, etc)

ROOTS

Some of the problems we encounter are because we are not grounded. Imagine roots going from your feet down into Mother Earth. Ask her to support you. Enjoy nature.

WHITE SHEET

Imagine a white sheet 20 feet below the foundation of your home, office, vehicle. Ask that any energy that is not the purest reflection of your higher self be picked up by the sheet and cleared.

Visualized the sheet picking up anything that needs to be cleared. See it moved through the home, office, vehicle and yourself. It will pick up thought forms, astral energies, left over emotions, electronic debris etc

Repeat this 3 times.

If it seems to get stuck at any time, explore what may want to stay. Invite it to know that it will get what it needs in the hands of the angels and that it is not wanted here any longer. This may be a time to ask for an essence to help with the clearing or an aroma-therapy product.

If it still doesn't clear, it may be time to ask for help with a profes-sional who can see the problem energy and will have more tools to address the issue.

COLUMN OF LIGHT

1. If you want to clear yourself.
2. Stand up.
3. Put yourself in a column of light.
4. Allow it to get brighter and brighter.
5. Breathe it in and out.
6. As you feel it more and more, allow it to intensify.

Imagine it burning out any impurities that might be in or around your body.

PRAYER

If you feel out of sorts or out of balance and you can't think of anything in your recent experience to cause those feelings, it may be something you picked up from someone around you. You may say this prayer as often as you'd like. Eventually, you will learn that it is often not your stuff. You will feel much more free when you learn how to let go of other peoples energy.

"May any energy that is not mine, be given what it needs and sent on to the light."

HUMAN CAR WASH OF LIGHT

1. Imagine a car wash set-up for humans.
2. As you walk into it, you are showered with light.
3. As you walk further, cleansing brushes gently scrub you clean.
4. Further in, you feel a warm wind some up and blow off anything you want to let go.
5. As you emerge from the cleansing, a robe of light is placed over you and protects you throughout the day.

GOLDEN VACUUM

Visualize a spinning vacuum that creates suction and removes anything that is not good for you. It can go up and down your body to clear out debris or all around the room to remove energy that is not good.

YA HAYY, YA HAQQ (pronounced ya hi, ya huck)

1. March in a circle, counter clockwise.
2. Raise hands to heaven drawing in good energy saying Ya Hayy (8 repetitions)
3. Quickly drop hands letting go of negative energy saying Ya Haqq (8 repetitions).
4. Do this to the count of 4
5. Then do it to the count of 2.
6. Then do it to the count of 1.

CHECKLIST FOR MAXIMIZING YOUR BRAIN

Life Style
- Remove Harmful Chemicals
- No Smoking
- Get more Sleep
- Limit your alcohol.
- No unnecessary drugs.
- Social engagements that you enjoy.
- Have achievable goals
- Learn something new outside your comfort zone

Exercise:
- Aerobic
- Stretch
- Brain Gym
- Eye exercise: push up, down, right, left
- Don't look at your feet when you walk, keep your eyes forward.

Thoughts:
- ANTS (automatic negative thinking)
- Affirmations

Supplements:
- Amino Acids
- GABA
- L-Glutamine
- Tyrosine
- DL-Phenylalanine

- 5 HTP
- L-tryptophan

Nutrients

- Antioxidants
- CoQ10
- Resveritrol
- Vitamin E
- Vitamin D
- Sam E
- St. Johns Wort
- Selenium

Water: ½ your body weight in ounces

Stress Relief

- Jin Shin Hands
- Alternate Nostril Breathing
- Toning the Chakras
- Affirmations
- Brain Merge
- Color Drain
- EFT
- Frontal Occipital Holding
- Flower Essences
- Healing Instrument
- Gratitude Journal
- Inner Child Work
- Forgiveness
- Reiki

DR JUDITH ORLOFF FROM HER BOOK SECOND INSIGHT

Quiz : Are You Intuitive?

1. Do you listen to your gut feelings about people?

2. Do you pay attention to your body's early warning signs such as fatigue, to take care of your health?

3. Do you listen to the wisdom of your dreams?

4. When you sense someone is an energy vampire who drains your energy do you avoid him or her?

5. In relationships do you listen to "beware" signs such as getting a sick feeling in the pit of your stomach?

6. Do you pay attention to the vibes that people give off, positive and negative?

7. Do you act on what moves and inspires you rather than only making decisions by what seems right on paper?

PROBLEM SOLVING CHART

(Dowse or muscle test the issues that need to be addressed)

Food Intolerance:

Wheat	Peanut Butter
Corn	Coffee
Dairy	Soy
Citrus	Additives
High Fructose Corn	Eggs
Syrup	Sugar
Peas	

Issues:

Nutritional Deficiencies	Psychic
Improve Gut Function	Past Life
Blood Issues	Soul Loss
Weight Loss	Bacteria/Virus/Fungus
Exercise	Candidiasis
Breathing Exercises	Fermented Foods
Jin Shin Jyitsu Self	Poor connection to
Treatment	Higher Self
Brain Work	Vitamin
Toxic Environment	Mineral
Mercury Amalgams	Herbs
Genetic	Amino Acids

Give Up:

Coffee

Sugar

Alcohol

Perfume

Electronic Interference

Change Cleaning

Supplies

Negative Thinking

Processed Foods

Particular Organ Function:

Liver

Kidney

Bladder

Ovaries

Gonads

Adrenals

Pancreas

Thyroid

Spleen

Heart

Prostate

Stomach

Intestines

Back

Lungs

Skin

Eyes

Ears

Modalities:

Reflexology

Massage

Lymph Drainage

Magnets

Biofeedback

TENS Unit

Kinesiology

NLP

Reiki

Shamanism

Flower Essences

Herbs

Acupuncture

Medical Doctor

Sleep Clinic

T'ai Chi

Qigong

Jin Shin Jyitsu

Color

Meditation

Air Purifier

Affirmations

Yoga

Therapeutic Touch

People and Processes:

Byron Katie

Colin Tipping

Deepak Chopra

Carolyn Myss

Richard Gerber

Julia Cameron

Julia Ross

Judith Orloff

Dr. Mercola

Wayne Dyer

Echart Tolle

Gay and Katie

Janet Heartson

Hendricks

Sandra Ingerman

Dr. Daniel Amen

Joan Borysenko, Ph.D

Belleruth Naparstek

Louise Hay

Donna Gates

Michaelle Small Wright

Harville Hendrix

Donna Eden

Gary Zukav

Trouble Managing Emotions:

Anger	Despair
Fear	Helpless
Hurt	Shame
Lonely	Outrage

Ownership of the Five Bodies:

Physical	Spiritual
Emotional	X-factor
Mental	

Relationships:

Mother	Siblings
Father	God/Goddess/Great
Spouse	Spirit

THE FAIRNESS PRINCIPLES: HOW TO CREATE A FAIRER SOCIETY AND A FAIRER LIFE FOR ME AND YOU

1. Make a vow today that even if life sometimes seems unfair, you don't have to be. Take a daily fairness inventory of your actions and drop those that are unfair.

2. Adopt the golden rule in your practices and your relationships. Do onto others as you would have them do unto you. Treat everyone with respect, fairness and honesty. Refuse to engage in any activity at another's expense.

3. Choose words and actions at work that are both good for you and good for the rest of the team.

4. Do not support any business that does not place fairness to the consumer above profits. Refuse to support any business that engages in corporate cheating or other practices that deliberately harm its competitors (such as predatory dumping).

5. Refuse to support any organization that engages in practices that are unfair to any sector anywhere in the world.

6. Support or work only for corporations or institutions with fairness principles for wage-setting, so that managers and CEO are not paid wages disproportionate to their contribution and workers in domestic or foreign factories are not paid disproportionately less than their contribution.

7. Support only those laws that provide equal opportunity and fair practices for all citizens of every persuasion, and lobby against any laws that blatantly favor one sector of society over another or that are blatantly unfair to any sector of society.

8. Refuse to support any financial institution or corporation with disproportionate rewards to its senior management, compared with rewards to its consumers.

9. Encourage fair play over winning at all costs in your children. Teach them to choose words and actions that benefit both themselves and those around them, even those that are not their friends.

10. Be respectful, considerate and fair with your neighbors and the members of your community, even on your own property. Please add your own ideas to this list and pass it on. Fairness is even more contagious than greed because in our hearts we know what's fair.

Lynne McTaggart   From her book The Bond

LETTING GO OF RIGHT AND WRONG

When we hold judgments of others, we use our energy in a way that is limiting. If we want to heal and clear our life of the burdens that have accumulated, we need to forgive and let go. Ask yourself these questions when faced with conflicts and old hurts.

1. What am I thinking about this situation that caused me harm?

2. What do I know is absolutely true? Facts, not feelings.

3. How did I contribute to the problem?

4. If I lower my shoulders, breathe and allow myself to energetically expand, can I let go of this issue?

5. Is there a lesson from my soul here? Did this incident bring up an old wound that needs attention?

6. How can I reframe this to see it as an opportunity for growth and

to see this person as an agent for my healing?

7. If I look from an objective place, can I see that I am not a victim, but am a participant in a healing for myself and the other person?

8. Do I need to process more feelings before I get to the gold of understanding?

This worksheet combines wisdom from Byron Katie, Colin Tipping, The Sedona Method and Huna.

LESSONS IN DEALING WITH CHRONIC PAIN.

1. Breathe into it. Consciously tense then release your muscles. It can ease the pain.

2. Befriend the pain. Try to imagine that there is a good purpose to the pain. What is it here to teach you? Have a conversation with it, write down what it says to you and journal about it.

3. Immerse yourself in pleasure. Take a yummy bath. Have a massage. Have an orgasm, it can temporarily override the pain and give you a break from it.

4. Release the emotional judgment and fear attached to the pain. Any emotional expression will help release stagnant energy that contributes to the pain. It is amazing how many negative thoughts we can have about it.

5. Laugh. When you laugh it creates endorphins which are natural painkillers.

6. Exercise. Pain is usually caused by stagnant energy. Move and it will ease the pain.

7. Cry. Having a good cry (yes, real men cry) can release a valium like substance in your system which eases pain.

8. Connect with friends. Socializing is good for the brain and good for the soul which may not get rid of pain, but certainly makes life more fun.

9. Cut back on alcohol and sugar. They create an acidic system which increases inflammation. Learn about alkaline foods.

10. Biofeedback works! Use it to manage the severity of the pain.

MYTHS THAT HOLD US BACK

Sensitives are often told as children that they are "too sensitive for their own good". As a child that frustrated me because there was nothing I could do about my sensitivities and so the statement was just meaningless. I needed support, not a statement designed to shut me down. I was overweight for most of my childhood. I think I was stuffing my feelings about "being too sensitive". As the story about my Dads motorcycle illustrates, I saved lives with my "sensitivities". Yet no one in my immediate circle of family and friends understood that part of me.

If you are the parent or friend of a sensitive child, please talk to them about how it feels. Please explore with them ways to manage those sensitivities, so they feel supported. There are groups they can attend, there are many websites that would be helpful. I think I would start everyone off with Doreen Virtues work. She is a psychotherapist that also experiences angels. She uses intuition in her work and teaches her clients how to do so. She has many books, cards, etc that will help sensitives feel they might have valuable skills.

We may have been told that other peoples thoughts can harm us. "They are too negative" is an example. Please be careful of this because it can cause you to feel victimized too often. Try finding a prayer or blessing to send to the "negative thinker" to make the situation feel better. You may also say to them, "I prefer to think of it in this way..." which can help them shift and help you fend off the negativity.

We sensitives may also feel we need to take on the pain of others. It does not help them and it does not help you. Please do the energy clearing techniques in this book to help you resist the urge to carry other peoples stuff.

In her book Second Sight, Judith Orloff, MD shares her struggle with accepting her gifts. She has gone on to develop ways to support sensitives. Her practice as a psychiatrist has grown immensely since she has claimed her intuitive abilities, shared it with her professional community and developed an informative website that covers many issues that empaths experience.

Cyndi Dale has a few books out that offer ways to use intuition in business. She is the president of Life Systems Services and provides intuitive based consulting for organizations and individuals.

COUPLES WORK : RELATIONSHIP BANKS

Rules for Sessions:

Listen without interrupting.

Reflect back what you heard.

Be willing to look at any pattern that causes you to react in anger or fear.

Use "I" statements: "When you do _____ I feel _____."

Relationships have accounts just like banks. What are you investing in your relationship bank accounts? Make your own lists to help you understand ways you are starving or feeding love.

Things that starve love:

Hiding the truth

Built up anger and resentment

Wanting to be right

Criticism and Praise

Making your partner your enemy

Holding grudges

Flirting-leaking sexual energy

Addictions

Silence

Not listening

Taking your partner for granted

Being a love martyr, sacrificing yourself

Controlling your partner

Disrespectful behavior

Playing the Blame Game

Negative list: (criticizing me in front of friends)

1.

2.

3.

4.

5.

6.

Things that feed love:
   Being Kind
   Telling the complete truth
   Writing a love letter
   Becoming a love team
   Gratitude
   Being committed to growing together
   Forgiveness
   Emotional, mental and physical fidelity

Living a healthy lifestyle

Communicating your feelings

Paying attention

Appreciating your partners value

Asking for what you want and need

Cooperating with your partner

Treating your partner with respect

Positive list: (appreciating my garden)

1.

2.

3.

4.

5.

6.

SEVEN STEPS TO SEEING A MIRACLE

1. Train yourself to see miracles. We see what we are used to seeing. If you begin a gratitude journal, you will train yourself to see miracles. Also, A Course in Miracles can help you retrain your mind to allow miracles. While taking the course I yelled :"If I create my reality, then I want to see a rainbow everyday for two weeks." Guess what! I saw a rainbow every day for those two weeks. They were in the sky yes, but also on key chains, t-shirts, bumper stickers and window decals. It was truly amazing.

2. Try thinking of yourself as a beautiful child of God and/or Goddess. Many of us have low self esteem, so we see the world through those eyes. You can retrain yourself to see the divine in you, then you will see the divine all around you.

3. Notice Nature. The natural world is full of beauty and that beauty is truly miraculous. Try looking at a budding rose, a nautilus shell, a sunset etc.

4. Learn to believe. If you don't believe, but would like to, simply state that you are willing to learn to believe. You don't have to be perfect right away, just be willing to learn.

5. Clear your heart. Your unexpressed emotions can block the light that you could see if you were seeing clearly. Allow yourself to express sadness, grief, anger and disappointment. Underneath those you will find your joy.

6. Be honest. Telling the truth really helps us see the truth. And

the truth is miraculous.

7. Change your set points. We have set points that define and limit who we think we can be. Try examining your set point about how much money you can earn, or how much weight you can lose or how much love you can receive. Then allow your set point to shift and recognize your unconscious is the only one limiting you. Dream what you look like inside, the abundance you feel and the great capacity to love that you possess. Allow these feelings to magnetize a greater you. For example, tell yourself every day that you choose to experience your abundant, thin and loving self.

What can you do to have a healthy brain?

Your brain is the most complicated, amazing organ in the universe! It controls everything you do, feel and think. Take care of it. Commit to better brain health this year and you will be glad you did. Dr. Daniel Amen has compiled the largest data base of brain scans in the world. His information has been the source for some of this article. Go to www.amenclinics.org for more information. My Kinesiology training and research prepared me to write and do presentations about brain function and ways to restore brain balance.

Some Brain facts:

Brains don't mature until age 25. So if your 18 year old acts immature, give him time.

We use much more than 10% of our brain and every neuron has a purpose.

There are more connections in the brain than there are stars in the universe.

Brain tissue the size of a grain of sand contains 100 thousand neurons and over 1 Billion synapses all talking to each other.

Our brain generates enough wattage to light a light bulb.

It is 80% water.

It weights approximately 3 pounds. Humans have the largest body to brain ratio.

Why work on having a healthy brain?

So we can:

feel good about ourselves.

be productive

avoid dementia & Alzheimer's

have a good memory.

have fun

Safety Suggestions:

Use scent free products and avoid exposure to chemicals.

Relax without drugs or alcohol: even a few drinks can be a problem.

Smoking seriously damages the brain because it inhibits circulation and breathing.

Avoid trans-fats

Wear seat belts and helmets

Best Practices

Water: ½ your weight in ounces daily. (Coffee and tea etc. do not count)

Eat from the rainbow: red cabbage, greens, broccoli, plums, strawberries, blueberries.

Take Omega 3 Fatty Acids and eat foods containing them: wild salmon, flax, sardines.

Physical Exercise: this is key to good circulation and therefore good brain health.

Brain Exercise: Learn something new

Socializing increases memory, adds new info

Move your eyes: up, down, side to side

Automatic Negative Thoughts: ANTS

Thoughts like: "I'm a failure." You can manage them by asking yourself if they are true. If you can't prove they are true, then let them go.

Replace with an affirmation that could be true such as "I learn from my mistakes".

If the thought pops up again, just let it go or repeat the positive statement.

Brain plasticity keeps your brain young:

Engage in new learning and experiences.

Eat a healthy diet and exercise

Wear sunglasses.

Eye movement is important.

Social Activity

Positive attitude

Be purposeful with focus & attention

Important Foods, supplements and spices

1. Eat from the rainbow: greens, red peppers, blueberries, strawberries, red cabbage etc
2. Omega 3 fatty acids: wild salmon, sardines, flax
3. CoQ10, L-Glutamine, multivitamin, selenium
4. Spices: turmeric, saffron, sage, cinnamon, basil, thyme, oregano, garlic, ginger and rosemary.
5. Walnuts, avocados, tomatoes, beans and soy.

The worlds most important question is "What have I done for my brain today?"

The list should look like this:

I rode my bike, hiked or went for a vigorous walk.

I ate my greens, took CoQ10, and bought a scent free laundry detergent

I learned something new.

May this information fill you with inspiration to take care of that beautiful brain of yours!

THE FOUR CLAIRS   (Doreen Virtue coined this phrase)

It can be helpful to identify what your usual clair is. It will help you to fine tune it and perhaps increase your capacity to recognize your gifts.

Clairvoyance (clear seeing) is related to your visions. It is represented by times when you see number patterns. You may have a vision like a dream or feel like you are actually seeing it with your physical eyes. You may have a fleeting image or movement in your peripheral sight. You might see something glow that needs to catch your attention, like a passage in a book or a winning ticket.

Clairaudience (clear hearing) is about your hearing. It can be a voice that you hear that is not connected to a body. It may be a story on the radio or from a neighbor that is the exact thing you needed to hear. It may be a whisper that guides you or a shout of warning. It could include hearing music that isn't from an obvious source or a high pitched ringing sound.

Clairsentience (clear feeling) is about your senses. You may smell a perfume or smoke. You may feel energy from someone or get a feeling that doesn't seem to come from any source around you. You will get hunches or gut feelings that cause you to feel things without any logical explanation. There maybe feeling out of the blue like joy or sadness. You could feel a touch out of nowhere or a change in air temperature.

Claircognizance (clear thinking) refers to knowing something without knowing how you know. It can be that "aha" moment when you realize how to fix something or why something happened. You may have wise words come through you for someone else, where you say just the right thing that they need to hear. You might say to yourself "I knew that" after something occurred.. like a feeling of deja vu. You may feel like you know someone and not know why.

I suggest that you simply be curious how these will manifest in your life and how the angels want to communicate with you. There is no need to be afraid you are crazy. We are Spirits having a human experience. Things of Spirit are important and essential to who we are. If communication becomes obsessive or combative then you may want to seek counseling to sort out the source of your experiences. But for the most part, trust your feelings, your heart, your inner voice, your visions, your knowing for they are the most important parts of who you are and will enhance your life.

Notes:

Notes: